D1260289

EDUCATION FOR ADOLESCENTS

[X]

FOUNDATIONS OF WALDORF EDUCATION

RUDOLF STEINER

EDUCATION FOR ADOLESCENTS

Eight lectures given to the teachers of the Stuttgart Waldorf School

JUNE 12–19, 1921

Translated by Carl Hoffmann

Anthroposophic Press

The publisher wishes to acknowledge the inspiration and support of Connie and Robert Dulaney

❖ ❖ ❖

This volume is a translation of *Menschenerkenntnis und Unterrichtsgestaltung*, which is vol. 302 of the complete works of Rudolf Steiner, published by Rudolf Steiner Verlag, Dornach, Switzerland, 1986.

Published by Anthroposophic Press
RR 4, Box 94 A-1, Hudson, N.Y. 12534

Library of Congress Cataloging-in-Publication Data

Steiner, Rudolf, 1861–1925.
[Menschenerkenntnis und Unterrichtsgestaltung. English]
Education for adolescents : eight lectures given to the teachers of the Stuttgart Waldorf School, June 12–19, 1921 / Rudolf Steiner ; translated by Carl Hoffmann.
p. cm. — (Foundations of Waldorf Education ; 10)
Includes bibliographical references and index.
ISBN 0-88010-405-8
1. Education—Philosophy. 2. Waldorf method of education.
3. Anthroposophy. I. Title. II. Series.
LB775. S72E287 1996
370".1—dc20

96-8224
CIP

10 9 8 7 6 5 4 3 2 1

Printed in the United States of America

Contents

Introduction

The present lecture cycle, given in Stuttgart in June 1921 at the opening of the upper or high school and now titled *Education for Adolescents*, is also known as the *Supplementary Course.* This name suggests quite clearly that the talks were meant as an expansion and continuation of the cycle *The Foundations of Human Experience,* which Steiner had presented to the teachers at the opening of the Stuttgart Waldorf (elementary) school two years earlier.[1]

Through these lecture cycles, Steiner advocated a consolidation of interest and interaction of all teachers in the curriculum and teaching methods in the lower and middle elementary schools. Repeatedly in the *Supplementary Course* lectures, we read that the teachers of the high school should share with their colleagues in the lower grades and kindergarten a common interest in the children's developmental stages in order to gain a meaningful and true picture of puberty and adolescence.

A meaningful study of the *Supplementary Course* must, therefore, be pursued against the background of the *Foundations of*

1. Previously titled *Study of Man,* this lecture cycle is now published as *The Foundations of Human Experience* by Anthroposophic Press, Hudson, NY, 1996.

Human Experience as well as in conjunction with the thoughts given by Steiner in other lectures to teachers.[2]

This overlap explains the almost aphoristic treatment received by some subjects in the *Supplementary Course.*[3] Rather than a systematic structure for education in the high school, the high school teachers are presented in the *Supplementary Course* with a sketch of the adolescent years that is permeated by spiritual science.

Steiner referred to this time—the time between the fourteenth and twenty-first years—as the third seven-year period, and he did not treat it as comprehensively as he did the second seven-year period. Frequently here, he describes the development of the young across several phases, often (in lecture seven, for example) even placing it in terms of cosmic connections. It is obvious that he wished to point out changes, metamorphoses, and polarities—above all, the incredible dynamics of all the events taking place during this period. We should not, therefore, view puberty and adolescence as an isolated age but as a condition for transition, as a transitory state of being, paradise having been lost and not yet regained. We could also refer to this third seven-year period as a river flowing between the banks of childhood and adulthood—appreciating its connection with both the preceding and following seven-year periods.

The 1965 translation of the *Supplementary Course* by the teachers of the Waldorf School in Sussex, England, was a great

---

2. Especially in the lectures: "The Healthy Development of the Physical-Corporeal as Basis for the Free Development of Spirit and Soul" (Dornach, December 23, 1921–January 7, 1922, GA 303); "The Fundamental Forces of Soul and Spirit in the Art of Education" (Oxford, August 8–25, 1922); "The Art of Education as Basis for an Understanding of the Human Being" (Torquay, August 12–20, 1924); "The Practice of Education from the Aspect of a Spiritual-Scientific Knowledge of the Human Being" (Dornach, April 15–22, 1923); "Methods of Teaching on the Basis of Anthroposophy" (GA 304).
3. Recorded in shorthand by a member of the audience.

service to the school movement. Its happy reception is evidenced by its many reprintings, and to the present the translation has continued valid.

Now, there are several reasons why the time has come for a new translation. For one thing, we have seen far-reaching changes in the organization of Waldorf schools. For another thing, we have witnessed a rapid expansion of the Waldorf movement in the Anglo-Saxon world. Due to the growing interest in Rudolf Steiner's impulse, many people who had not previously heard of anthroposophy have come into contact with Waldorf schools. Consequently, a careful introduction by way of such basic books as the *Supplementary Course* has to be considered.

During this time, people in English-speaking countries have thoroughly investigated the issue of translating anthroposophical works. They have earnestly considered the problems of recreating Steiner's style and idioms in other languages without losing the specific elements of his thought structure. Many translations have in fact sounded too German for the English-language reader—a problem that complicates comprehension.

Questions concerning high school in particular have become ever more pressing in English-speaking countries in recent years. In the United States, there are many schools educating children through the first eight grades that have been in existence for over twenty years. And many of these schools are now considering the possibility of expanding, of adding the high school grades.[4]

Steiner's more generally given indications for the high school led some people to believe that this phase of education allowed for a great amount of freedom regarding the choice of subjects

---

4. In 1995, there were more than a dozen Waldorf schools in the United States considering the addition of the high school grades.

and teaching methods, that the foundation of an understanding of the human being was here not so important. This is certainly not the case. For it is especially at this time in the human biography that artistically structured lessons must be brought into line with a knowledge of the spiritual origin of the young. Since we have but few directions from Steiner, we are given the awesome task of examining the content and methods of our teaching in regard to their spiritual validity.

These recent decades have brought fundamental changes in the nature of adolescence and in the ways this age is dealt with—changes, that is, not only for the young themselves but also for their environment. During this time, the young become conscious of their individuality—a painful process. During this ever more difficult process of individuation, something occurs—a flicker of light, a half-conscious, often delicate and tentative experience of questions concerning one's very own destiny and tasks in life.

We can perceive in the adolescents of today a duality that did not exist in the past. On the one hand, they evidence a far greater awareness, a deeply conscious feeling of responsibility for the world as well as themselves. On the other hand, the path to their individual tasks, to the realization of their selves, is accompanied by far greater pitfalls and dangers—which may trip them up, cause them even to lose the ground under their feet. The path for today's adolescents is threatened from both sides by temptations—some hidden, some quite open. Are these threatening dangers the effect of the acute, heightened consciousness?

Of one thing, at least, we can be certain. The current and future generations will especially need understanding adults during adolescence—will need them as partners, as friends, as helping teachers. An enthusiastic teacher, in trying to understand the innermost impulses of the young during this stage of their lives, will develop a quite new love for them. I believe that this love is the condition for a positive relationship of the young to the older generations, so that the young will no longer withdraw from the world of the adults, resigned to the belief that that world demands too much of them in the way of adapting to home, school, and environment. Very few young people today are ready and willing to choose this path of adapting. And those who do choose this path ultimately do so from a feeling of frustration.

In considering the questions regarding our adolescents, we may again become students ourselves, willing to learn. This is one of the basic conditions for Waldorf education. Our students will only learn from the adult who also chooses the path of learning.

The *Supplementary Course* gives us descriptions of archetypal processes that allow the teacher to gain insights into the interesting dynamics of human biography, insights into the mysterious chemistry involved in the search for the self.

* * *

My special thanks to Carl Hoffmann. His readiness to accept the difficult task made the publication of a new translation possible.

—*Hans-Joachim Mattke*

1

STUTTGART / JUNE 12, 1921

My dear friends:

After almost two years of Waldorf education, and in view of the opening of yet another important class in September, we shall again consider a number of curriculum issues. I shall, however, leave this till tomorrow. Today I shall take a look at the results of our work so far. New ideas may arise from this review that could further improve our teaching.

In order to prevent a possible misunderstanding of what I am going to say today, I can assure you that I have noticed and appreciated the progress made during these two years. The way you are teaching—the presentation of subjects—is already such that it can be said: You have progressively come to grips with your tasks. You have, in an extraordinarily healthy way, fused with the goals of these tasks.

But it behooves us to consider such details as can provide the basis for a positive development of our work. I believe that in reviewing your work, all of you will have this initial feeling that our work with the children has kept helping us to improve our methods. There is, however, something we might have missed—perhaps with a degree of pain. It is relatively easy to mediate the subject matter to the children, to give them a momentary understanding for what we teach them. But we have not yet succeeded in making the subject matter last for them, in making it a part of their whole being, so that it can stay with them throughout their lives, so that we may achieve the same results with our teaching as with our talks at special festive occasions.

Our teaching must live. It must reach beyond the ideas, images, feelings, and skills the children have acquired. We must give them something that can—depending on their dispositions and possibilities—continue into their adult lives.

Just as the limbs of any living creature are developing during the growing stages, are becoming bigger and more complicated, so also should the ideas, feelings, and skills we give our children be not fully formed but rather capable of growth and development. We must see to it that our teaching does not remain rigid, static, but that it can grow with them, change as they change during the course of development, so that at the age of thirty or forty they will still have the benefit of what they learned at seven or eight, because the learning has grown and developed as their complicated limbs have developed, because it has slowed down at the appropriate time, and so forth.

Our teaching must enter the children's being deeply, so that it can continue to develop with them, can live or fade away. This means that the children will have to absorb whatever we present to them and make it their own. The question arising from this realization is: How can we achieve this? The answer will come from assumptions quite different from those we generally make.

My dear friends, what we need to do is to make every effort at understanding the human being in his or her totality—in our case, this is the child—as a being consisting of body, soul, and spirit. Such understanding will allow us to comprehend the inner processes in the children when we teach them various subjects, and, as a result, we shall learn to adjust our work to these processes. Today, therefore, we shall concentrate on gaining a complete picture of how we ought to teach and educate.

To begin, let me draw your attention to the many erroneous ideas that are current regarding the human being. Teachers, especially, are convinced that what and how we teach—be it through visual perception or stories or activities—will increase children's skills, ideas, and concepts, will strengthen their feeling, and that the increase and strengthening will last throughout the children's lives. But this is not so. Let us proceed by example. We give the children certain ideas and mental images—in a history lesson, in the history of literature, in mathematics, or in geography—assuming that they will retain them as lasting possessions. It is generally assumed that such concepts descend somewhere into the lower regions of the soul, into the sub- or unconscious spheres, and that there they remain in one way or another, to be called upon whenever a situation arises. This is the function of memory, so they say.

But this assumption is not true. The ideas, the mental images, which we produce in the children and which, with us, they elaborate and develop, immediately change when the children occupy themselves with other things after the lesson. In no way does a concept swim about in the unconscious in its original form, to be called up at random. This is certainly not the case. The ideas and concepts we produce in the children are, when the children are no longer thinking about them, no longer present anywhere. They are not swimming about; they are no longer there. The process by which children later recollect is quite different from what is generally assumed—namely, that the ideas and concepts are called forth from the unconscious.

Not only may the processes taking place in recollecting and perceiving be compared; in a certain respect, they may be considered as one and the same. When we perceive something, when in the case of children we direct their soul activity to some outer object and develop with them an idea or concept, the activity will certainly be the children's very own; they are preoccupied, are working with the idea or concept. We call this process perception.

When the children remember something, the same process is involved, but now it is directed inward. Something is happening within the children. The children are working with, developing, something in the same way as in the perception of an outer object. These inner processes that continue when the original mental images of perception are no longer directly present are extremely complicated. It is very difficult to describe in any specific instance how a mental image prepares to reconnect with the human being in order to emerge as memory—so that the image may again be perceived, this time as an inner event. But when we remember, we really perceive inner events in the same way we perceive outer objects.

It is really not all that important to have an exact knowledge of these processes. We need to be aware of something else. We need to know that the continuing effects of mental images and ideas that, later, emerge in memory actually take place in the sphere of our feelings. It is our life of feelings—with its joys, pains, pleasures, displeasures, tensions, and relaxations—that is the actual vehicle for the enduring qualities of the ideas and mental images that we can recall at a later stage. Our mental images change into stirrings of feeling, and it is these stirrings of feeling that we later perceive and that enable us then to remember.

It is important for us to understand this process because we must pay special attention to it in education. If in line with the convictions of most teachers today, we merely present to the children things to be looked at, to be accurately perceived by the senses, we are not giving them anything that will help them to remember later in life. Their memory will be greatly enhanced, however, if we put feeling into our words, if we teach with warmth, if we spice our lessons with the possibility of allowing the children to experience corresponding emotions, if we make them smile or feel sad, if we endeavour to go beyond the merely intellectual aspects to the life of feeling.

I cannot overemphasize the importance of such an approach. It is, of course, more difficult. It demands great presence of mind. Mere intellectual instruction is easier than a teaching that wishes to stimulate the children's feeling, that makes for an inner connection with a subject. We need not be pedantic in this teaching, need not necessarily always connect feeling directly to the subject taught. We may refer to something else in order to stimulate feelings. The important thing is that the children's feelings are engendered during a lesson. Such stirrings of feeling aid memory. And this fact we must not lose sight of. Even in the driest of subjects, such as physics or geometry, we should try to appeal to the children's feelings. If, for example, we interrupt a thought process and ask a child, "If you were to do this and something unexpectedly were to happen ...?"—we add feeling to the lesson. We add tension, expectation, and relaxation that will permeate and benefit the thought process.

Never underestimate the effect of the unknown or half known. The effect of such on feeling is extremely important. If toward the end of a lesson we say, "and tomorrow we shall do this..."—the children need not know anything about "this"; their expectation and curiosity will still be aroused. If, for example, I have taught the properties of the square before those of the triangle and I conclude the lesson by saying, "Tomorrow we shall learn about the triangle"—the children do not yet know anything about the triangle, but it is exactly this fact that causes a certain tension, an expectation of what is to come, a looking forward to the next day's lesson. The effect will carry the day. We ought to make use of the unknown or half known in order to facilitate the children's effort at fitting the details into a totality. We really must not ignore such matters.

As we get used to working in this way we shall, on the one hand, in a quite elementary way, connect teaching with education and, on the other hand, feel the need to make ourselves ever more familiar with the nature of the human being, the child. And then, as out of our anthroposophical knowledge we ponder this nature, this wisdom of the human being, much will become clear to us and lead to increased teaching skills.

Developing such wisdom and teaching skills will ever more be of the gravest importance. It will allow the subject matter to fuse with the children, to become their very own possession. We have not yet achieved enough here.

Essentially our lessons consist of two interacting parts. We instruct, we exhort the children to participate, to use their skills, to be physically active. Be it in eurythmy, music, physical education, even writing or the mechanical processes in arithmetic—we try to engender activity. The other part of our lessons is concerned with contemplation. Here we ask the children to think about, to consider the things we tell them.

Although these two aspects always interact, they are fundamentally different. It is not generally appreciated how much the teacher of a contemplative subject, such as history, owes to a colleague who is more concerned with skills and aptitudes. Concentrating merely on contemplation leads the children to a stunted, prosaic adult life, with a tendency to boredom. They will have a superficial view of life, will not feel inclined to observe accurately, will not pay attention to events around them. Children who are trained predominantly in contemplation become benumbed, confused adults. We really owe a great deal, as teachers of contemplative subjects, to the teachers of handwork, music, and eurythmy. We can go so far as to say that the history teacher actually lives off the music or singing teacher and that, vice versa, the singing and music teachers live off the contemplative elements in history, and so forth.

In a situation that calls for directing the children's attention to something of a contemplative nature, when they are sitting on their chairs listening to and concentrating on a story or on something that demands their judgment—however great our efforts may be to get them to think for themselves, if they merely sit and listen, this is no more than, if I may use the paradox, a "waking sleeping activity." The children are, in a certain sense, outside the body with the soul and spirit, and it is only because the separation is not as complete as in sleep that the body's participation continues. Indeed, especially during a contemplative lesson, we can observe the same phenomenon that is present in sleep—namely, an ascending organic activity. In children who are merely listening to stories, organic processes are called forth that are identical to those occurring during sleep, when the metabolic processes ascend to the brain. Making the children sit and listen, we engender in them, in the organism, a delicate sleeplike activity.

It is generally assumed that sleep strengthens and replenishes the organism. Waking up with a headache could correct this view. We must be clear about the fact that the unhealthy parts of our organism are kept back by the awake activity of the upper organs, so that they cannot ascend. But during sleep they rise, ascend. And this rising upward of what is amiss in the organism is continuously engendered by our insistence on making the children listen, think, and contemplate. When, on the other hand, we teach them eurythmy, when we make them sing, or play instruments, when we employ them in physical activities, as in handwork and gymnastics, even when we make them write something—when they are in fact doing things, the organic processes thus stimulated are an intensification of waking activity.

Even if the effect is not noticed, singing and eurythmy are hygienic, even therapeutic activities. This cannot be denied. This hygienic, therapeutic activity will perhaps be the healthier the less we approach it in an amateurish medical way, the more we simply do it out of our healthy imaginative conception of life.

Still, it is good for the teachers to know that they cooperate as partners, that the children owe the healthy ascent of their body fluids—essential during a contemplative lesson such as history—to the singing or eurythmy lesson of the previous day. We can only benefit from such a comprehensive overview of education, which will encourage us, should a problem arise, to cooperate with our colleagues. We shall discover that we can advise each other if, for example, as a teacher of history I can discuss a child with the music teacher.

Little, if anything, will happen if this consultation takes place in a didactic, routine way. Positive results will be achieved only when—from the comprehensive overview—we feel the urge to discuss a problem with a colleague. Then we may be convinced that when the physics teacher notices a problem and talks it over with the singing teacher, the problem will be lessened or solved when the appropriate steps are taken in singing. The singing teacher will know better what to do than the physics teacher and will be grateful to that teacher for having drawn attention to the problem. Only in this way will we establish a fruitful cooperation as teachers. Only in this way will we be enabled to consider the totality of the human being. The rest will follow, one thing developing from another.

This greater mobility in education will result also in something we cannot do without—humor. We need humor not only for thinking, at the right moment, of the unknown or half known, through which we evoke tensions and relaxations as memory aids, but for something else as well. As we make our teaching ever more mobile, as we get used to considering the whole human being instead of merely the subject matter, we shall in time learn to enlarge certain aspects of our lessons. This widening of subject in all directions is again of enormous importance, especially when it occurs in the direction I shall shortly speak about.

Consider a physics lesson. We are certainly not in favor of having apparati in our classrooms or of methodically developing experiments. Such methods can be employed, can even be very intelligent. It could be asserted that such an approach has proved itself and that a great deal is achieved by it. But the effect is short-term, and we cannot be concerned merely with short-term effects. What we intend to do is to provide the children with something that will benefit them throughout life. To succeed in this intent, we have continuously to enlarge concepts. We must, of course, teach the phenomena in optics and hydraulics. But we must also learn to be ready, at appropriate moments, to relate certain aspects of lessons to other things in life.

Let me give you an example. We could, at a given opportunity, spontaneously refer to the weather, to climatic conditions, to phenomena occurring across the globe in a distant country, so that the students realize that there are connections everywhere in the world. They will then experience the feelings that arise when we are led from one phenomenon to another; the tensions and relaxations that result will allow them to identify with the subject, grow together with it, make it their very own possession.

The most important connection we can establish is the one with the human being. We should never miss an opportunity for making this connection. Every situation—be it during a discussion of an animal, of a plant, or of the phenomenon of warmth—every situation presents an opportunity, without losing sight of the subject, without diverting the students from it, to connect with the human being. What, indeed, is there to prevent us, when talking about the phenomenon of warmth, from mentioning fever? What is to prevent us, when talking about elastic balls in physics, from mentioning the phenomenon of vomiting, a process similar to the repulsion in elastic balls? Vice versa, what is there to prevent us, during a lesson on reflexes in the human organism, from mentioning the simple phenomenon of repulsion in elastic balls, and so forth?

Such connections to life in general can be established already in the lower grades, can gradually get the children used to seeing the human being as the confluence of all world phenomena. When we teach the things that lie outside the human being as natural phenomena, they will always tend to be forgotten. When, on the other hand, we relate them to the human being, when we consider the corresponding phenomena in the human being, we shall notice another tendency: that it is really impossible to regard something that is connected with the human being without feelings. We cannot describe the functions of the ear or of the heart without evoking feelings in the children. By relating the outer world to the human being we always stimulate their feelings—and this is so very important.

Making this connection is, therefore, so very important in subjects treating the objective world, subjects that are usually taught "objectively," as unconnected with the human being. We should always try to find such connections, and in fact, the most objective subjects are the ones that lend themselves most easily to our doing so, because all the world can be found within the human being.

Again, we have the means of aiding the children's memory. We can be quite sure that the children will soon forget facts learned by rote in physics. They will not identify with them; the facts will not become inner possessions. But as soon as we relate such facts to the human being, demonstrate what is happening for the human being, the facts will remain, will become an intrinsic part of the children's experience. What is explained to the human being about the human being becomes the human being's very own possession. It is necessary for us to avoid abstractions, on the one hand, and on the other hand, what Schlegel referred to as the "crude-material-concrete." Both should be avoided, especially in our lessons and education.

Let me give you another example. Recently I observed a lesson on comedy and tragedy in class eight. It is relatively easy to think of quite persuasive definitions of the comical, the humorous, the tragic, the beautiful, and so on. They can be found in current literature. But most, if not all, of them are abstractions and will not allow living mental images to arise. What actually happens is that our experience of a tragic, a sad event affects our metabolic processes, slows them down. Our experience of tragedy is, indeed, connected with our physical processes, as though something in our stomach cannot be digested, cannot pass into the intestine.

A deeply sad experience has the effect of literally hardening our metabolism, even though these processes are delicate. Indeed, if you happen to be unhappy, sad, or depressed, you are working against your digestion. The experience is identical to the feeling one has when food lies like a lump in the stomach, a crudely material but qualitatively comparable phenomenon.

In a healthy digestion, the food passes naturally from the stomach to the intestine, is absorbed by the villi, passes into the blood, then penetrates the diaphragm, so that it can be distributed in the upper organism. This physical process is, qualitatively understood, identical to the effect of laughing, when we artificially induce the vibrations of the diaphragm. Laughing is a process that makes us organically healthy; its effect is similar to that of a healthy undisturbed digestion.

Such knowledge will allow us to relate the humorous to the digestive processes. We are learning to think in the way the ancient Greeks did, are beginning to understand the Greeks' concept of hypochondria, of abdominal ossification. An objective observation will confirm this connection. Living toward the upper organism, getting the diaphragm into movement, stimulated by a healthy digestion and passing to the world outside—this physical process does, indeed, provide the connection of a humorous, happy mood to the physical body. By avoiding such abstract explanations as "humor allows us to rise above a situation," we shall succeed in establishing the confluence of the abstract with the concrete. We establish a totality. We show the children how to combine, in their minds, spirit and soul with the physical, corporeal. We repress the absolutely harmful modern ideas of continuously teaching the human cultural aspects—soul and spirit—without relating them to the physical and, vice versa, at the other pole of the pendulum, of speaking about the physical in crudely materialistic ways. Taken separately, neither approach is truthful; for the ideas interact, flow into each other.

It behooves us to evoke total, comprehensive ideas and images, by binding humor and tragedy not to abstract concepts but to the diaphragm. A possible objection is that doing so might encourage a materialistic view of the world. This is certainly not so. It is exactly by showing how spirit and soul are living in the physical that we bring people to the point of seeing that the whole of the material world owes its existence to soul and spirit. As soon as we can imagine—when somebody is laughing, when somebody experiences laughter in the soul and spirit—that the event is connected with the diaphragm, we shall also gradually arrive at the idea of the effects of spirit and soul in rain, thunder, and lightning. We are led to these realizations by relating everything to the human being.

In relating everything to the human being it is important not to dwell too much on the egocentric—because much or exclusive self-interest, egocentricity, would result in contemplative egotism. If, on the other hand, in our contemplative lessons, we connect everything to the human being, we produce in the human being—simply by making one see oneself as consisting of body, soul, and spirit—a disposition that provides the best basis for one's working from the depths of one's being during physical activities. If our lessons allow the contemplative thinking elements to connect with the human being, we shall educate our students through history, geography, physics to become singers, to become truly musical people. Affecting our students in such a way that we let them think what they themselves physically want, we produce something in them which we really ought continuously to be creating.

In order to achieve this creation, we must acquire certain concepts. As you well know, it is not possible to remain well fed without the need of eating again. We cannot feed a person and say: "This is it, you need no longer be hungry!" Living processes proceed in rhythms. This truth applies to music, to everything in life. A human being must live in rhythmic alternations, so that one's "being led back to oneself" is subjected to the highest tension and, in turn, to relaxation. The concepts we teach our students about stomach, lungs, and liver will produce in them a disposition that will again be offset in singing, in the way hunger alternates with eating—a rhythmic process. Only rhythm maintains life. The correct handling of the contemplative subjects will produce faculties that will correspondingly manifest in the other subjects.

If instead of merely enumerating Julius Caesar's actions, successes, and failures, we would at the same time give the children imaginative pictures of the man, paint as it were a historical situation, so that the children feel impelled to have in their imagination a kind of shadowy picture of him, see him walk, follow his walk in their minds—if they were to imagine Julius Caesar in such a way that they did not merely copy the image in a painting but actually modeled it in their minds, and if they then proceeded to a handwork lesson, you may be absolutely sure that they would knit better than they would have without Caesar.

Such connections are as mysterious as those between hunger and satiation. Ignoring the connections produces different results. For example, if we teach for an hour without stimulating the imagination of the children, their stomachs will be filled with acid, will have excessive pepsin. This cannot be avoided in a contemplative lesson. It is, however, not only a matter of acidifying the food in the stomach; there is also a spiritual dimension. All matter is at the same time spirit. When the children are singing, the pepsin's role is to produce in them the inner prickling they should feel during singing. This prickling cannot occur if the pepsin remains stuck in the folds of the stomach. And it does remain there if one only talks, without stimulating the imagination. When the imagination is stirred, the pepsin is distributed throughout the body, with the result that the singing teacher will be confronted by children whose organs are permeated by this prickling, this effervescent sensation. Without such experience—especially in the speech organs—the children will be lethargic and lazy, and they will sing without enthusiasm.

I tell you these things so that you can appreciate the importance of considering the totality of the school organism, of seeing it as a unit. Interfering in things that do not concern one does not help. Of course, each teacher must feel free to do what he or she thinks best. But one will gradually acquire the necessary skills by studying the nature of children and by appealing to their imagination. The children long for this attention, need it. And the teacher will greatly benefit from a preoccupation with this aspect of education.

A lively interest in human nature is, of course, the condition for succeeding in this endeavor. Such interest can be developed, and anthroposophy will provide you with all the hints you need. What I especially recommend to you—from a direct pedagogical/didactic point of view—is that you avoid getting stuck in abstractions when you develop your own concepts. You should instead endeavor to understand the human being in regard to organization.

You must actually become pioneers in a certain sphere, must tell yourselves: "We have today, on the one hand, the abstract sciences—history, geography, even physics, and so on. They are practiced in the most abstract ways. People acquire concepts. On the other hand, we have the sciences of the human being—anatomy, physiology—by means of which we learn about the human being, as though the organs were cut out of leather and reassembled." Truly, as cut from leather—because there is really no difference between the descriptions of living organs presented by our anatomists and cut-out leather pieces. The human being is not described as a totality. The spirit is ignored.

You can, however, be pioneers. You can contribute positively to education by making use of both the abstractions, the lifeless concepts propagated today, and the crudely materialistic approach. You may teach both, but only in order to combine them in a living way, by interweaving them. You could teach history in such a way that it enlivens anatomy, and anatomy in order to bring life to history. The function of the liver could, for example, give you an idea for treating the history of the later Egyptian culture, because the nuance, this special nuance in the presentation, the (let me say) aroma one has to spread across the later stages of Egyptian history, one acquires during the contemplation on the function of the liver in the organism. The effect is the same.

By interweaving subjects in this way you will not only give humanity something that is culturally interesting; you will also meet an educational need by bringing together the so-called physical, which does not as such exist, and the abstract spiritual, which again has no meaning as such. Thus you may enter the classroom in such a way that your words carry weight and, at the same time, acquire wings. You will not torture the children with words that merely fly away, nor will you teach them skills and aptitudes that weigh them down.

2

STUTTGART / JUNE 13, 1921

In yesterday's introduction I wanted to show the importance of the teacher's understanding of the human being and of the school as organic unit. Everything else really depends on this understanding. Today I shall touch on several issues that may then be further developed.

If we wish to have a correct picture of the human being, what really matters is that we rid ourselves of all the prejudices in the current scientific world conceptions. Most people today—even those who are not materialists—are convinced that the processes in logical thinking are carried out by the soul, an inner organism, and that the brain is used as a kind of mechanism for carrying out these processes. All logical functions and processes, they say, are cerebral. The attempt is then made to explain these processes in three stages—the forming of mental images, judgments, and conclusions. It is true, is it not, that we must apply these processes in our lessons, that we must teach and practice them?

We have been so conditioned to this way of thinking that all logic is a function of the head that we have lost sight of the real, the actual nature of logic. When we draw people's attention to the truth of the matter they demand proofs. The proof, however, lies in unprejudiced observation, in discovering the development of logic in the human being. Of the three stages—mental images, judgments, conclusions—only in the first is the head involved. We ought to be conscious of this: The head is concerned only with the forming of mental images, of ideas, and not with judgments or conclusions.

You may react by saying that spiritual science is gradually dismissing the head and diminishing its functions. But this is in accordance with the truth in its most profound meaning. The head really does not do all that much for us during our life between birth and death. True, in its outer appearance, its physical form, it is certainly the most perfect part of our body. But it is so because it is a copy of our spiritual organism between death and rebirth. It is, as it were, a seal, an impress of what we were before birth, before conception. Everything that was spirit and soul impressed itself on the head, so that it represents the picture of our prenatal life.

It is really only the etheric body—besides the physical—that is fully active in the head. The astral body and the I fill the head, but they merely reflect their activity in it; they are active for their own sake and the head merely reflects this. In the shape of the head we have a picture of the supersensible world. I indicated as much during last year's lectures when I drew your attention to the fact that we are really carrying our heads as special entities on the top of our bodies. I compared the body to a coach or horse and the head to the passenger or rider. The head is indeed separated from the world outside. It sits, like a parasite, on the body; it even behaves like a parasite. We really must get away from the materialistic view of the head that attaches too much importance to it. We need our head as a reflecting apparatus, no more. We must learn to see the head as a picture of our prenatal spirit and soul organism.

The forming of mental images and ideas is indeed connected to the head. But not our judgments. These are actually connected to arms and hands. It is true—we judge with our arms and hands. Mental images, ideas we form in our heads. But the processes leading to judgments are carried out by the mechanism of arms and hands. The mental images of a judgment do, as its reflection, take place in the head.

You can develop a feeling for this distinction and then recognize its important didactic truth. You can tell yourselves that the task of our middle organism is to mediate the world of feelings. The rhythmical organism is essentially the basis for the mediation of feelings. Judgments are, you will agree, deeply related to feelings, even the most abstract of judgments. When we say "Carl is a good boy," this is a judgment, and we have the feeling of confirmation. The feeling of confirmation or negation—any feeling actually that expresses the relation between predicate and subject—plays a major role in judgments. It is only because our judgments are already strongly anchored in our subconscious that we are not aware of our feelings' participation in them.

There takes place for us as human beings, inasmuch as we judge, a phenomenon that we must understand. The arms, although in harmony with the rhythmic organism, are at the same time liberated from it. In this physical connection of the rhythmical organism with the liberated organism of the arms, we can see a physical, sense-perceptible expression of the relation between feelings and judgments.

In considering conclusions, the drawing of conclusions, we must understand the connection to legs and feet. Our contemporary psychologists will, of course, ridicule the idea that it is not the head that draws conclusions but the legs and feet. But it is true. Were we, as human beings, not oriented toward our legs and feet, we could never arrive at conclusions. What this means is that we form ideas and mental images with the etheric body, supported by the head organism; we make our judgments—in an elementary, original way—with our astral body, supported by our arms and hands; and we draw conclusions in our legs and feet—because we do this with our ego, and the ego, the I, is supported by legs and feet.

As you can thus see, the whole of the human being participates in logic. It is important to understand this participation. Our conventional scientists and psychologists understand but little of the nature of the human being because they don't know that the total human being is employed in the process of logic. They believe that only the head participates in it. We must now understand the way in which the human being, as a being of legs and feet, is placed on the earth—a way quite different from that of the human head being. We can illustrate this difference in a drawing.

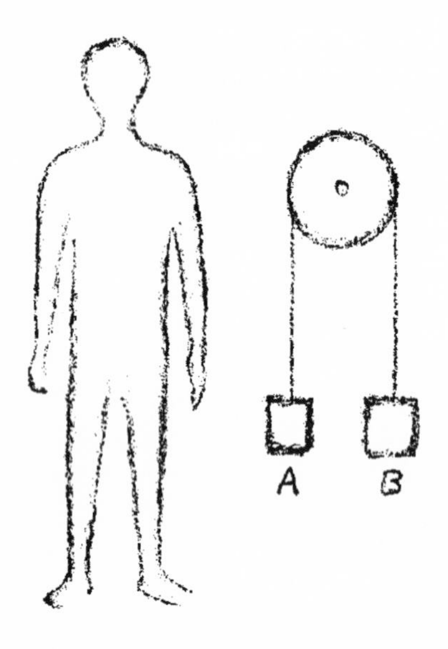

By imagining the outline of the human being we may arrive at the following concept. Let us assume that the person in the diagram is lifting a weight by hand, in our case a heavy object weighing one kilogram. The object is lifted by hand. Let us now ignore the person and, instead, tie the object (A) to a rope, pass the rope over a pulley, and tie another object of either identical or heavier weight to the other end (B). If B happens to be heavier, it will draw the original weight (A) up. We have here constructed a mechanical device the achievement of which is identical to that of hand and arm. I can replace hand and arm with a mechanical device—the result is the same. I unfold my will and, in so doing, I accomplish something that can equally be achieved by some mechanical device, as shown in the illustration.

What you can see in this diagram is a happening that is quite objective. The employment of my will does not alter the outer picture. With my will I am fully placed into the objective world. I impart myself into the objective world; unfolding my will, I no longer differentiate myself from it.

What I have demonstrated can be observed especially clearly when I take a few steps or use my legs for something else. What the will accomplishes during the use of my legs and feet is a process that is quite objective, something that takes place in the world outside. As seen from without, there is no difference between a mechanical process and my own personal effort of will. All my will does is to direct the course of events. This is most strongly the case when I employ functions that are connected with my legs and feet. I am then really outside myself, I flow together with the objective world, I become part of it.

The same cannot be said of the head. The functions of the head tear me away from the world. What I call seeing and hearing, what ultimately leads to the forming of ideas and mental images, cannot in this objective way impart itself to the world outside. My head is not part of that world; it is a foreign body on earth, a copy of what I was before I descended to earth.

Head and legs are extreme opposites and, between them, in the center—because there the will is already active, but in conjunction with feelings—between them we have the organization of arms and hands. I ask you to keep in your mind this picture of the human being—through the head, as it were, separated from the earth, having brought the head from the spiritual world as a witness, the proof of belonging to the spiritual world. One imparts oneself into the physical world by adapting the organs of will and the feelings to the outer laws, to environment and institutions. There is no sharp boundary between outer events and the accomplishments of the will. But a sharp boundary is always drawn between outer events and the ideas and mental pictures mediated to us through the head.

This distinction can give us an even better understanding of the human being. The head develops first in the embryo. It is utter nonsense to regard it as being merely inherited. Its spherical shape tells you that it is truly a copy of the cosmos, whose forces are active in it. What we inherit enters the organism of our arms and legs. There we are our parents' children. They relate us to the terrestrial forces. But our heads have no access to the earth's forces, not even to fertilization. The head is organized by the cosmos. Any hereditary likeness is caused by the fact that it develops with the help of the other organism, is nourished by the blood that is affected by the other organism. But it is the cosmos that gives the head its shape, that makes it autonomous and individual. Above all, the work of the cosmos—inasmuch as it is connected to the head—can be seen in those things that are part of the nerve-sense organism. We bring our nerve-sense organism with us from the cosmos, allowing it to impart itself into the other organism.

This knowledge is important because it helps us to avoid subscribing to the nonsensical idea that we are the more spiritual the more we ignore the physical and to avoid talking in abstractions about spirit and soul. We become truly spiritual when we learn to see the connection between the physical/corporeal and the soul and spirit, when we understand that our head is a product of the cosmos, is organized by it, makes us part of it. The organism of our legs is inherited; there we are our parents' and grandparents' descendants.

This knowledge, being true, will affect our feelings, while all the current concepts—be they about spirit or matter—are abstract, in no way related to reality. They leave us cold, cannot stir our feelings. I would therefore like to ask you to take to your hearts, to ponder deeply, and to develop for your educational work the fact that there is really no difference whether the human being is regarded as a physical/corporeal being or as a being of spirit and soul. Once we have learned to observe spirit and soul in the correct way we shall see them as creative elements from which flows the physical/corporeal. We shall recognize spirit and soul in their creative activity. And if, as artists, we reflect on this activity in the right way, we shall gradually lose sight of the material altogether as it becomes spirit all by itself. The physical/corporeal transforms into spirit in our correct imagination.

When one stands firmly on the ground of spiritual science, of anthroposophy, it no longer matters if one is a materialist or a spiritualist. It really doesn't matter. The harm done by materialism is not the study of material phenomena. If this study were performed thoroughly, the phenomena would transform into spirit and all the materialistic concepts would be recognized as absurdities. The harm done is the feeblemindedness that results when we do not complete thought processes, when we do not concentrate enough on what the senses perceive. We thus lose sight of reality. If we were to pursue thoughts about the material world to the end, we would arrive at the picture, the idea of the spirit.

As for spirit and soul, as long as we enter their reality when we reflect on them, they will not remain as the abstractions we are given by our current sciences but will assume form, will become visible. Abstract understanding becomes an artistic experience that will ultimately result in our seeing spirit and soul as material, tangible reality.

Be one a materialist or a spiritualist both perspectives will lead to the same result, provided the thought process is completed. Again, it is not the spirit that is the problem in spiritualism but rather this uncompleted thought process that so easily turns the spiritualist into an idiot, a nebulous mystic, a person who causes confusion and who can only vaguely come to grips with reality.

There is yet another essential and important task for you. Equipped with a sound understanding of the nature of the child, you must develop an eye for distinguishing the child with a predominant cosmic organism from the one with a predominant terrestrial/physical organism. The former will have a plastically formed head, the latter a plastically structured trunk and, especially, limbs.

What now matters is to find the appropriate treatment for each. In the more earthly child, the hereditary forces are playing a major role; they permeate the entire metabolic limb system in an extraordinarily strong way. Even when the child does not appear to be melancholic, there is, nonetheless, alongside the apparent temperament a nuance of melancholy. This is due to the child's earth nature, the "earthiness" in the child's being.

When we notice this trait in a child, we shall do well to try to interest him or her in music that passes from the minor to the major mood, from the melancholic strains of the minor to the major. The earthly child especially can be spiritualized by the movements demanded by music and eurythmy. A child with a distinct sanguine temperament and delicate melancholic features can easily be helped by painting. And even if such a child appears to have but little talent for music or eurythmy, we should still try our best to develop the disposition for it that is certainly there.

A child with a distinctly pronounced head organism will benefit from subjects such as history, geography, and the history of literature. But care must be taken not to remain in the contemplative element but, as I already pointed out yesterday in another context, to evoke moods, feelings, tension, curiosity that are again relaxed, satisfied, and so on.

Again, it is a matter of habitually seeing the harmony between spirit and body. The ancient Greeks had this knowledge, but it got lost. They really always saw in the effects of a work of art on human beings something they then also applied to the physical. They spoke of the crisis in an illness, of catharsis, and they spoke in the same way of the effects of a work of art and of education. The Greeks observed the processes that I described yesterday, and it is up to us to rediscover them, to learn to unite soul and spirit with the physical/corporeal in our thinking.

It is thus important that we use all our own temperamental energies, in order to teach history with a strong personal accent. Objectivity is something the children can develop later in life. To worry about objectivity, when we tell them about Brutus and Caesar, at the expense of expressing the feeling engendered in us during the dramatic presentation of their differences, their polarities—this would be bad teaching. As teachers, we must be involved. We do not need to wax passionate, to roar and rage, but we do need to express at least a delicate nuance of sympathy or antipathy toward Caesar and Brutus in our characterization. The children must be stimulated to participate.

History, geography, geology, and so on must be taught with real feeling. The latter subject is especially interesting—to feel deeply about the rocks beneath the earth. Goethe's essay on the granite can here be of great help. I strongly recommend it to you. Read it with feeling, in order to see how a person could humanly relate—not merely in thinking, but in his whole being—to the primal father, the age-old, holy granite. This approach must, of course, then be extended to other subjects.

If we cultivate these responses in ourselves, we shall also make it possible for the children to experience and participate in them. This is naturally a more difficult approach, as it takes greater effort. But our teaching will be alive, a living experience. Believe me, everything we mediate to the children via feelings allows their inner life to grow, while an education that consists of mere thoughts and ideas is devoid of life, remains dead. Ideas and thoughts are no more than mirror images. With them we merely address the head, whose value lies in its connection with the past, its time in the spiritual world. When we give the children images and ideas that are made living through our strong feelings, we make a connection to what is significant for the earth, to the elements contained in the blood.

Let me give you an example. It is absolutely necessary for us to develop the appropriate feeling for the hostile, destructive forces in an airless space. The more graphically we show this—after the air has been pumped out—the more dramatically we can describe this terrible airless space, the more we shall achieve. In earlier times people referred to it as *horror vacui.* They experienced this horror streaming from it; their language contained it, and we must learn to discover this feeling again. We must learn to see a connection between an airless space and a thin, dried up person. Shakespeare indicated this in *Julius Caesar:*

> Let me have men about me that are fat;
> Sleek-headed men and such as sleep o'nights:
> Yond Cassius has a lean and hungry look;
> He thinks too much: such men are dangerous.

It is the well-padded whom we trust, rather than the lean, skinny, bald-headed person with cold intellect. We must feel this relation of a lean person or a spider to airless space. Then we shall be able to pass on to the children, through imponderables, the cosmic feeling that must be an integral part of the human being.

Again and again, when speaking of education, we must emphasize the necessity of connecting the totality of the human being to the objective world, because it is only then that we can bring a healthy element also to those aspects in education that are so harmfully influenced by materialistic thoughts. We cannot, my dear friends, be as outspoken as Herr Abderhalden who—after having been invited to a eurythmy performance where in my introduction I also mentioned the hygienic and other aspects of physical education—said: "As a physiologist I cannot see anything in physical education that is physiologically justified. On the contrary, physical education is, in my opinion, the most harmful activity imaginable; it has no educational value whatsoever. It is a barbarity."

We cannot afford to be so direct. We would be attacked from every side, as happens today. It is so, isn't it, when you really think about it, that all the exercises and activities of physical education, wherein the worst of materialistic concepts are applied to the physical body, have become idols, fetishes—be they systems concentrating on the strongly physical, the superphysical, or the subphysical; be it the Swedish method or the German. What the systems and methods have in common is the belief that the human being is no more than a physical organism—a belief resulting from the very worst ideas developed by the age of materialism, not in accord with the thoughts I have outlined.

The exercises are generally based on an assumption describing the ideal posture for the human being—the correct curvature of the spine, the form of the chest, the manner of moving the arms and hands. What we actually get from the exercises is certainly not a human being but merely the picture these people have made themselves of the human being. No wonder there are so many diagrams in the manuals. This picture of the human being lends itself to being modeled in a papier-mâché figure. Everything that is said of the human being in Swedish gymnastics can be found in such a papier-mâché doll. The living human being can then be used like a sack and made to imitate the lifeless dolls. The real human being is ignored, is lost sight of in such practices. All we have are papier-mâché figures.

In spite of the fact that they have become so popular and influential, these practices must be seen as infamous, really quite reprehensible, because of this exclusion of the real human being. The human being is theoretically excluded in the sciences; in modern gymnastics the human being is practically excluded, reduced to a papier-mâché figure. Such practices should never find their way into education. In good physical education, the students should only carry out movements and assume postures that they can also actually experience within. And they do experience them.

Let's take a look at the breathing processes. We must know that we must bring the children to the point where the breathing-in bears a faint resemblance to tasting some favorite food. This experience should not go so far as to the actual perception of taste but merely to a faint resemblance of it; the freshness of the world ought to be experienced when breathing in. We should try to get the child to ask: "What is the intrinsic color of the air I am breathing in?" We shall indeed discover that as soon as breathing is correctly experienced, the child will have the feeling that "it is greenish, really actually green." When we have brought a child to the point of experiencing in-breathing as greenish we have accomplished something. Then we shall also always notice something else: that the child will ask for a specific posture when breathing in. The inner experience stipulates the correct corresponding posture, and the right exercises will follow from it.

The same procedure will lead to the experience of the corresponding feeling in breathing out. As soon as the children, when breathing out, can feel that they really are fine, efficient boys and girls, as soon as they experience themselves as such, feel their strength, ask to apply their strength to the world outside, then they will also experience, in a way that is healthy and appropriate to their age, the corresponding abdominal movement, the movement of the limbs and the bearing of the head and arms. This rich feeling during breathing out will induce the children to move correctly.

Here the human being is employed. We can see the human being before us, no longer allowed to be a sack, imitating a papier-mâché figure. We are moving in accordance with the soul that then pulls the physical body after it. We adapt the physical movements to the children's needs, to their inner, soul and spirit experience.

In the same way, we should encourage the inner experience the children's physical nature asks for in other areas—in the movements of arms and legs, in running, and so forth. We can thus really connect physical education directly to eurythmy, as it should be connected. Eurythmy makes soul and spirit directly visible, ensouls and spiritualizes everything that moves in us. It makes use of everything human beings have developed for themselves during their evolution.

But—also—the physical can be spiritually experienced. We can experience our breathing and metabolism if we advance far enough in our efforts. It is possible to do this—to advance to the point that we can experience ourselves, including our physical organism. And then, what the children are—on a higher level, I would say—confronting in eurythmy can pass into physical education. It is certainly possible to connect the two activities, to build a bridge from the one to the other. But this kind of physical education should be based on the development of movements not from the mere experience of the physical/corporeal but rather from the experience of soul and spirit, by letting the children adapt the physical/corporeal to their experiences.

Of course, in order to achieve this we ourselves must learn a great deal. We must first work with these ideas before we apply them to both ourselves and especially before we apply them to our teaching. They don't easily impress themselves on our memory. We are not unlike a mathematician who cannot remember formulae or theorems but who, at a given moment, is able to redevelop them. Our situation is the same. We must develop these ideas about the total human being—spirit, soul, and body—and we must always make them livingly present. Doing so will stand us in good stead. By working out of the totality of the human being we can have a stimulating effect on the children.

Again and again you will find that when you have spent long hours in preparing a lesson, when you have grappled with a subject and then enter the classroom, the children will learn differently than they would when taught by a "superior" lecturer or instructor who spent as little time as possible in preparation. I actually know people who on their way to school quickly read up the required material. Indeed, our education and teaching are deeply affected by the way we grapple not only with the immediate subject matter but also with all the other things connected to skills and methods. These things, too, should be worked and grappled with.

There are spiritual connections in life. If we have first heard a song in our mind, in the spirit, it will have a greater effect on the children when we teach it to them. These things are related. The spiritual world works in the physical. This activity, this work of the spiritual world, must be applied especially to education and didactics. If, for example, during the preparation for a religion lesson, the teacher experiences a naturally pious mood, the lesson will have a profound effect on the children. When such a mood is absent, the lesson will be of little value to them.

3

STUTTGART / JUNE 14, 1921

In today's lecture we shall consider how the content of a lesson may be adapted to the life of the children. There can be no doubt whatsoever that an education that is not based on a true understanding of the human being cannot possibly succeed in adapting the content of a lesson to the reality of human life.

The spiritual aspect of the human being is not recognized today; it is really only the physical body that is considered. There are some, perhaps, who admit to something of a soul nature that, in a vague way, influences the physical body. But even they do not consider the inner concrete nature of soul and spirit. It is exactly this consideration that anthroposophy is to contribute toward an understanding of the human being. It is only this that will, in a conscious way, make the adaptation of our lessons to the human life processes possible.

Let us assume—it will not be difficult to imagine it—that the children are listening to a story you tell them, or that they are looking at a picture you drew for them on the blackboard, or that they are looking at a diagram of an experiment, or that they are listening to a piece of music you play for them. In each of these activities you are initially in a relation to the outer physical reality of the children. But what you are inserting into the children in a roundabout way through the physical reality—be it through the eyes, the ears, or the comprehending intellect—everything that is thus placed into the children very soon assumes a quite different form of life.

The children go home, they go to bed, they go to sleep; their egos and astral bodies are outside their etheric and physical bodies. What you did with the children in this roundabout way through the physical body and also the etheric body continues in the astral body and the ego. But the latter two are now, during sleep, in a quite different environment. They experience something that can only be experienced during sleep, and everything you taught the children participates in the experience. The effects of the lesson that remain in the astral body and ego are part of the experience during sleep. You must know that you let flow into the astral body and ego what you teach the children through this detour of the physical body and that you thus affect the children's sleep experience. The children will present to you on the following morning the results of what they experience between falling asleep and waking.

A simple example will clarify this for you. Let us think of a child who is doing eurythmy or singing. The physical body is active, and the active physical body and the etheric body impress this activity on the astral body and ego. The ego and astral body are forced into participating in the movements of the physical and etheric bodies. But they resist, because actually they have other forces to concentrate on. These forces must now, in a way, be subdued. And although the ego and astral body resist, they must accept what their own physical and etheric bodies mediate to them—in eurythmy it is more the physical body; in listening to a piece of music, it is more the etheric body.

Ego and astral body then enter the world we live in between falling asleep and waking up. Everything that has been impressed on them continues during sleep to vibrate in them. Ego and astral body actually repeat—in the more intricate and spiritualized way peculiar to their nature—what they experienced in eurythmy and music. They repeat all of it. And what they thus experience during sleep, this the children take with them to school on the following day. The children incorporate the experience into their etheric and physical bodies, and we have to reckon with that.

Considered in totality, the human being presents an extraordinarily complicated structure for us to come to terms with in our lessons. Let us now take a closer look at these processes. Let us consider a child who is doing eurythmy. The physical body is in movement, and the movements of the physical are transferred to the etheric body. Astral body and ego initially resist, but the activities of the physical and etheric bodies are impressed on them. Astral body and ego then separate during sleep and connect the impressions to spiritual forces that are quite different. On the following morning astral body and ego return the impressions to the etheric and physical bodies. We can then see a remarkable harmony between that which was received from the spiritual world during sleep and what the etheric and physical bodies experienced during eurythmy.

The effect shows itself in the way the sleep experiences adjust to what was prepared and carried out on the previous day. It is only in this complementing of the physical/etheric by the spiritual that we can see the special healing element of eurythmy. Indeed, spiritual substantiality is brought to the human being upon awakening in the morning after a day including eurythmy.

It is similar in singing. When we let a child sing, the essential activity is that of the etheric body. The astral body must strongly adapt to this activity and, again, initially resists before taking it into the spiritual world. The astral body returns, and what it brings back again expresses itself in effectively healing forces. We may say that in eurythmy we have a force that mainly affects the health of the child's physical body, while in singing a force expresses itself that mainly affects the child's mechanism of movement and, through movements, then again the health of the physical body.

We can make very good use of these connections in education. If we organize our curriculum—this is an ideal, but the teachers could at least try to come close to it—so that the eurythmy lesson is given in the afternoon, it will be allowed to continue its life during the following night. On the next day, we can teach a physical education lesson in the way I outlined yesterday. The experience then penetrates the body in such a way that the movements made in physical education have a healing effect. Much can be achieved by this alternation of eurythmy and physical education.

Or again, much can be achieved on any one day when we let the children sing. They take this experience into the spiritual world during sleep. On the following day we let them listen to music—we let them listen to rather than make music. What was done on the previous day is then consolidated in the listening to music—an extraordinary healing process. You can see that under ideal conditions—that is, a curriculum structured to adapt to the conditions of life—we can affect the children's health in an extraordinary way. We shall do still far more in this regard.

Let us take the physics lesson as another example. We make an experiment. Remember what I said yesterday: Our thinking, our mental pictures, are head processes, while it is the rhythmic human being who judges, and the metabolic human being who draws conclusions. It is especially our legs and feet that draw conclusions. If you keep this in mind, if you think of the processes of perception in this way, you will tell yourselves that everything connected with the will, everything we produce out of ourselves during the process of perceiving, is deeply connected to the drawing of conclusions and not only to the forming of mental pictures or ideas. When I look at my body, then this body is itself a conclusion. The idea, the mental image, arises only because I am looking at my body, but in carrying out a definite half-conscious or unconscious procedure, I synthesize the parts in a way, akin to the forming of judgments, that allows me to experience the totality. I then express the experience in the sentence: This is my body. But this is already the perception of a conclusion. As I perceive, perceive intelligently, I am drawing conclusions. And the whole of the human being is within these conclusions.

This is so during an experiment, because in experimenting the whole of the human being is active, receiving information. Conclusions are continuously drawn during the process. Judgments are generally not perceived; they are predominantly inner processes. We may thus say that the whole of the human being is occupied during an experiment.

From an educational point of view, children do not really benefit much at all from such experiments. They may be interested in what they see, but their normal organization as human beings is as such not strong enough for them to exert themselves continuously in every part of their being. That is not possible. I always ask too much of them when I ask them to exert themselves totally. The children always get too far outside themselves when I ask them to observe an experiment or something in the environment. The important aspect in education consists in really paying attention to the three parts of the threefold human being—in allowing each part to receive its due, but also in getting all to the point where they can correspondingly interact.

Let us return to the physics lesson. I make an experiment. The whole of the human being is occupied, is asked to make an effort. This is quite enough to begin with. I then draw the children's attention away from the instruments I experimented with and repeat the various stages. Here I am appealing to their memory of the direct experience. During such a review or recapitulation—without the presence of the apparati, purely in the mind—the rhythmic system is especially enlivened. After having engrossed the whole of the human being, I now appeal to the rhythmic system, and to the head system, because the head naturally participates during recapitulation. The lesson can then be concluded. After first having occupied the whole of the human being, then mainly the rhythmic system, I dismiss the children. They go to bed and sleep. What I activated in the whole of their being, then in their rhythmic system, now during sleep continues to live in their limbs when astral body and ego are outside the body.

Let us now regard what remains lying on the bed, what allows the content of the lesson to keep on working. Everything that has developed in the rhythmic system and the whole of the human being now streams upward into the head. Pictures of these experiences now form themselves in the head. And it is these pictures that the children find on waking up and going to school. Indeed, it is so. When the children arrive at school on the following morning they have, without knowing it, pictures of the previous day's experiments in their heads, as well as pictures of what—in as imaginative a way as possible—I repeated, recapitulated after the experiment. The children I then confront have photographs of the previous day's experiment in their heads. And I shall now reflect on yesterday's lesson in a contemplative way. Yesterday I experimented, and in reviewing the experiment I then appealed to the children's imagination. In today's lesson I add the contemplative element. In doing so, I not only meet the pictures in the children's heads, but also help to bring the pictures into their consciousness.

Remember the progression: I teach a physics lesson, make an experiment, then recapitulate the stages of the experiment without the apparatus. On the following day, we discuss the previous experiment, contemplate it, reflect on it. The children are to learn the inherent laws. The cognitive element, thinking, is now employed. I do not force the children to have mere pictures in their heads, pictures they have brought with them from sleep, pictures without substance, without meaning. Just imagine the children coming to school with these pictures in their heads, of which they have no knowledge. If I were to immediately start with a new experiment, without first nourishing them with the cognitive, contemplative element, I would again occupy the whole of their being, and the effort they would have to make would stir up these pictures; I would create chaos in their heads. No, above all, what I must do first is consolidate what wishes to be there, provide nourishment. These sequences are important; they adapt to, are in tune with, the life processes.

Let us take another example, a history lesson. In the teaching of history there is no apparatus, no experiment. I must find a way of again adapting the lesson to the life processes, and I can do this as follows. I give the children the mere facts that occur in space and time. The whole being is again addressed just as during an experiment, because the children are called upon to make themselves a mental picture of space. We should see to it that they do this, that they see what we tell them, in their minds. They should also have a mental picture of the corresponding time. When I have brought this about, I shall try to add details about the people and events—not in a narrative way, but merely by characterization. I now describe and draw the children's attention to what they heard in the first part of the lesson. In the first part, I occupied their whole being; in the second, it is the rhythmic part of their being that must make an effort. I then dismiss them.

When they return on the following day they again have the spiritual photographs of the previous day's lesson in their heads. I connect today's lesson with them by a reflective, contemplative approach—for example, a discussion on whether Alcibiades or Mithradates was a decent or an immoral person. When I make an objective, characterizing approach on the first day, followed on the next day by reflection, by judgments, I shall allow the three parts of the threefold human being to interact, to harmonize in the right way.

These examples show what can be done if the lessons are properly structured, if they are adapted to life conditions. The structuring and adaptation are only possible in our curriculum, which allows the teaching of a subject for several weeks. They are not possible in the traditional schedule, wherein physics is taught on one day and, perhaps, religion on the next. How could one thus consider what the children bring with them? It is difficult, of course, to structure all the lessons in this way, but one can at least come close to doing so. And by taking a good look at our schedule, you will see that we have attempted to make that possible.

It is furthermore also important to have an overview of all these connections. If you remember what I said yesterday—that it is not only the head but the whole human being who is a logician—you will learn to appreciate the significance of activities that require skills. It really was not a mere whim on our part when we introduced knitting also for boys. The faculty of judgment is indeed essentially enhanced by this activity of the hands. It is least developed through mere logical exercises. Logical exercises actually do very little for the development of the faculty of judging, of forming opinions. By connecting predicate to subject we contribute nothing to that faculty. What we actually do in that instance is make the faculty of judgment rigid. Children so exercised will grow into adults who can only judge according to patterns or schemes. Too many intellectual exercises result in schematic individuals. Another result of such exercises is too much salt deposit; the human being is permeated by salt and tends toward perspiring. We can easily observe this in children whose judgments have been unduly taxed: they perspire too much during the night.

Indeed, it is true. When we are too strongly and one-sidedly intellectual/spiritual—without knowing that the physical/corporeal is the pure expression of the spiritual—we usually affect the body, and mostly in the wrong way. Herbart's education, as well as that of others—education that is predominantly based on developing the faculty of forming mental images and ideas—results in the destruction of the body. It is important for teachers to know this.

You can see the significance of what I have told you in other areas of life. Every decent human being is supposed to listen to sermons in church. This is certainly a good tradition. The usual sermons are rather abstract. In fact, the preacher is trying to direct his congregation from everyday life to higher regions. They are to be edified and so on. It is all quite justified. Still we must understand what is actually happening during today's sermons, preached by people who are living in abstractions, who are ignorant of the connections in nature, whose thoughts do not contain such connections, who in fact do not even enjoy natural phenomena.

Let us now assume that the faithful attend such sermons that are not connected to everyday life. There are many such sermons nowadays. The faithful listen. Initially we do not notice anything amiss. But they do get physically ill, albeit only to a slight degree that is outwardly not noticeable. The effect of such sermons is the breeding of slight illnesses. A few hours after such a sermon, the listeners are subjected to the processes of an illness. The pain is consciously experienced to only a half or even a quarter degree. The inevitable effect is the feeling of one's miserable body. But surely the cause cannot possibly be in the sermon that has raised one to higher, more spiritual regions! One then analyzes one's feelings, becomes contrite, and realizes: I am a sinner. This is the interpretation of the illness that follows a sermon. And this—making the congregation experience themselves as sinners—may even have been intended by a certain unconscious shrewdness on the part of the sermonizer.

This phenomenon, quite general in our time, is connected with the other phenomena of decadence. I have mentioned it in order to show you that a wrong preoccupation with the spirit does not affect the spirit but rather the body, and quite concretely; I have mentioned the phenomenon so that you may understand that we ought to educate our children from a knowledge of this accord of the spirit with the physical body.

Sometimes curious events are not noticed, although they greatly influence the whole of our cultural life. During the last third of the nineteenth century less attention was given to the teaching of geography. The subject of geography played an ever diminishing role in teachers colleges. It was given an unimportant place in the curriculum, to be taught as a secondary subject by either the teacher of history or the teacher of the natural sciences. But take another good look at our diagram of the human being on the blackboard. When we see the human as a being who draws conclusions, who is placed within the world and does not separate from it through the head, we cannot think of him or her without the surrounding space. Space is part of the human being. Insofar as we have feet and legs, we are a part of the world of space. And the teaching of geography is, spatially considered, for the astral body a "being-put-on-its-legs." The astral body actually grows denser and thicker lower down. We teach about space and in so doing increase the density of spirit and soul in the lower astral body, toward the ground. In other words, we consolidate, we bring about a certain firmness in the human being when we teach geography in an imaginative way—always stressing the reality of space, making the children conscious of, for example, the distance between the River Thames and Niagara Falls.

If we teach geography clearly and graphically, we place the human being within space, and we especially cultivate an interest in the whole world. The effects will be seen in various ways. Individuals taught geography in this way will have a more loving relation with their fellow beings than those who have not learned about spatial relationships. They learn to take their place next to other human beings, learn to be considerate. These things strongly affect the moral life, whereas the neglect of geography results in an aversion to loving one's fellow beings. Even a superficial observation will confirm this. The connections are there, even if they are not noticed. Today's unhappy cultural phenomena are the effects of such follies.

The effects of the teaching of history are quite different. History is concerned with time. We only teach it correctly when we pay attention to this fact. If we merely concentrate on historical episodes, we do not consider the time element enough. If, for example, I speak about Charlemagne as though he were the children's uncle who is still alive today, I give them a false picture. Whenever I speak of Charlemagne, I must give the children a clear and graphic experience of the distance in time. I can do this by saying: "Just imagine—you are a small child and you take your father's hand." The children will have no difficulty in imagining this. I now point out the difference between the child's and the father's ages. I continue: "Your father holds his father's hand, then he your grandfather's, and so on. Now imagine thirty people holding hands. The thirtieth could be Charlemagne." In this way, the children get a feeling for the distance in time. It is important to teach history in this way—not placing isolated episodes next to each other but rather giving the children the feeling of distance in time.

It really is important to point out the characteristic differences [in consciousness—*translator*] when we deal with specific epochs in history, so that the children can have an idea of them. What matters is that historical events are seen to be living within the framework of time. Seeing historical events in this way strongly affects our inner life.

If, on the other hand, we teach history in a way that ignores the time element and also takes hold of the inner life too strongly—that is, if we concentrate on recent local history at the expense of events in the distant past, if (as it were) we put the emphasis in our lessons on cultivating a wrong patriotism (you will easily think of many such instances)—then we shall greatly engender obstinacy and willfulness of the inner life and a tendency toward moodiness. These are side effects, which will, above all, make people reluctant to observe world events objectively. And this is so terrible today. Neglecting geography and taking the wrong approach to history have greatly contributed to the serious illnesses of our time. You yourselves will admit to the problems you have in facing many a situation now, problems resulting from the way you were taught history in school.

The examples I have given you will illustrate the path our teaching must take if it is to connect to life conditions, to life impulses, in a healthy way. We cannot be satisfied simply with mediating facts; we must, above all, be aware of the life conditions of the human being in the physical, soul, and spiritual connections. We must always see the human being before us; and we must see the human being in his or her totality, as a being who is also extremely active during sleep. If we ignore this sleep activity—and this is ignored in today's education, apart from the hygienic aspects of sleep—if we ignore the fact that the content of our lessons continues into sleep, develops further during sleep, we will have the quite definite effect of making the human being into a robot, an automaton.

We could, indeed, venture to say that today's education is in many respects an education not toward humanness but toward the most obvious type of human automaton—namely, the bureaucrat. Our children are trained to become bureaucrats. Such people are no longer really human. They are fixed, they have an existence, they are finished. The human being is lost, is concealed behind the label. We have an appointment with an officer, be it a clerk or barrister, and it matters little who the actual person behind the label is.

Such is the result of only paying attention to daytime consciousness in education, of denying the spiritual element, of not considering the activities during sleep. We see this tendency in a frightening way in modern philosophy. Descartes and Bergson assert that the ego constitutes the continuity of the human being, that in the ego we can grasp the reality. I would like to point out to such people that they then cease to exist as soon as they fall asleep, that they always begin life anew on waking up. The dictum "I think, therefore I am" should really be changed to: "On June 2, 1867, I was from 6 A.M. to 8 P.M., because I thought during that time. Then again I was from 6 A.M. to 8 P.M. on the following day." Life would then become rather complicated. What lies between 8 P.M. and 6 A.M. would have to be excluded. But this is not considered, because such people prefer all sorts of ideas and abstractions to the realities at the basis of the human being.

But we must deal with these realities in our education. Doing so will allow us to educate human beings again. Doing so we need not then worry about establishing the right social or economic conditions. People who have been educated as human beings will see to them. Clearly, cultural life must be autonomous and independent. We can educate human beings only when concentrating on their human aspects, when we think about social change merely as a consequence of such an education—that is, not as having been made by the government. Cultural life must not be an appendix of the state or of economic life but must develop out of its very own sphere.

4

STUTTGART / JUNE 15, 1921

Our talks so far will have shown you the necessity of including exact knowledge of the physical human being when you prepare your lessons. The reason we consider such apparently remote matters is the important step our school is taking in adding a tenth grade class to the present elementary grades. In the tenth grade class we shall have girls and boys who are already more mature, who are at an age that will have to be treated especially carefully. I would like to spend the next few days in giving you a thorough understanding of this age when, as you know, important developmental stages occur.

You may well say that this is surely the business only of those who teach at this level. But this is not so. The teachers in our school must develop ever more into a complete organism, and all of you will, directly or indirectly, be concerned with all age groups, with the total education of every child.

However, before I address myself to the needs of the fourteen-, fifteen-, and sixteen-year-old students, I must today touch on some preliminary matters. During our meetings we shall then work on the tenth grade curriculum.

Let us, therefore, continue in the way we began during the last two days. I would like to impress on you the connection between the spirit/soul and the physical/corporeal aspects of the human being, especially of the child. Today's culture regards spirit and soul merely intellectually. Our cultural life does not include an actual and living spiritual life. And in the mainly Catholic central European countries, Catholicism has assumed forms that are no longer true, so that even there one cannot expect any help regarding the religious mediation of spiritual life. The Protestant spiritual life has become more or less fully intellectualistic. As far as our school is concerned, the actual spiritual life can be present only because its staff consists of anthroposophists. We do not teach anthroposophy—our school must not represent a world conception—but through the way the teachers are acting, through their inner life, the soul and spirit elements enter the school as though through the imponderables of the soul.

When we now teach the various subjects expected of a school—reading, the thought processes in arithmetic, those in the natural sciences, everything that is of a cognitive nature—we give the children ideas and mental pictures. The ideas and mental images are for the child's organism an activity that is quite different from physical/corporeal instruction—which, although it participates in the education of the thought processes, is also carried out independently. Physical/corporeal instruction is carried out quite independently in eurythmy, in physical education, and in instrumental music, but no longer in singing. Everything is, of course, relative. But there is a great difference, a polarity, between what the children are asked to do in these subjects—and also when they are learning reading and writing, when we strongly appeal to the physical activity—and what they are asked to do in subjects such as arithmetic, in which case the physical activity plays a subordinate role. In handwriting, on the other hand, physical activity plays a predominant part.

We should really go into details. Let me single out the subject of writing and show you the role physical activity plays. There are two types of people in regard to writing. (I believe I have already mentioned this to those of you who have attended previous lectures.) There are those who write as though the writing is flowing from their wrists. The forming of the letters is carried out from the wrist. Future business people are actually trained to write in this way. Their writing flows from their wrists, and this is all there is to it. That is one of the two types of people in regard to writing. The other type is disposed to looking at the letters. These people always contemplate what they write, deriving an almost aesthetic pleasure from it. These are the painter type, and they do not so much write from the wrist. Those of the first type do not paint.

I actually got to know the special training for people who are prepared for business. They are encouraged to put a kind of flourish to the letters. Their writing is characterized by continuous flourishes emanating from a certain swinging motion of the wrist. Taken to an extreme, this kind of writing will lead to something that is really quite awful. I know people who carry out all sorts of swinging motions with their pens in the air before they begin to write—a quite terrible thing when taken to an extreme.

We really ought to get people to write in a way that is akin to painting. Writing in that way is far more hygienic. When writing is accompanied by an aesthetic pleasure, the mechanical aspect is pushed into the body. It is the inner organism rather than the wrist that is writing. And this is most important, because the mechanical aspect is then diverted from the periphery to the whole of the human being. You will notice that when you teach children to write in this painting way, they will also be able to write with their toes. This would, in fact, constitute a triumph, a success—when a child is able to hold a pencil between the toes and form adequate letters. I do not say that this ability should be developed artistically. But we do have in such an instance a shifting of the mechanical activity to the whole human being. You will agree that in this regard most of us are extremely clumsy. Can you think of anyone who is able to pick up a piece of soap from the floor with his or her toes? To do this at least should be possible. It sounds grotesque, but it points to something of great significance.

We should cultivate this painting-like writing. It pushes the actual mechanical activity into the body, and the writer's connection to the writing is brought to and beyond the surface. The human being is imparted into his or her environment. We should really get used to seeing everything we do, rather than doing things thoughtlessly, mechanically. Most people do write mechanically, thoughtlessly. Because writing is thus a many-sided activity, we can, in a certain way, consider it as a significant aspect in our lessons. In arithmetic, on the other hand, the actual writing has a subordinate position, because with that subject it is the thinking that preoccupies the student.

We must now be quite clear about the processes taking place during reading. The activity of reading is initially spiritual and then continues into the physical body. It is especially the activities that are of a cognitive, mental/spiritual nature that considerably tax the delicate parts of the physical organization. You can picture, physiologically, the deeper parts of the brain, the white matter. The white matter is the actual, the more perfectly organized part of the brain. It is organized toward the more functional tasks, whereas the gray matter at the surface—which is especially well developed in humans—provides the brain's nourishment. The gray matter has remained behind, in a very early stage of evolution. In regard to evolution, it is the deeper part of the brain that is more perfect.

If we teach a child to observe well, as in reading, we greatly tax the gray matter, engendering a very delicate metabolic process. And this delicate metabolic process then spreads throughout the organism. It is especially when we believe ourselves to be occupying the children mentally and spiritually that we affect their physical organism most strongly. The observation and comprehension during the reading of and listening to stories engender metabolic processes that tax the children to an inordinately strong degree. We could call what is happening the impression of the spiritual into the physical. A kind of incorporation of what we observe and comprehend during a story is necessary. Something akin to a physical phantom must develop and then impart itself into the whole organism. The organism is filled with delicate salt deposits. Not coarsely, of course. A salt phantom is imparted into the whole organism, and the necessity arises to dissolve it again through the metabolism.

This process takes place when the children read or listen to stories. When we believe ourselves to be occupying the mind and spirit in our lessons, we really evoke metabolic processes. And this must be considered. We cannot do anything else but to see to it that our stories and reading material are faultless in two respects. First, the children must be interested in the subject. Genuine interest is connected with a delicate feeling of pleasure that must always be present. That feeling expresses itself physically in very subtle glandular secretions that absorb the salt deposits caused during reading and listening. We must endeavor never to bore the children. Lack of interest, boredom, leads to all sorts of metabolic problems. This is especially the case with girls. Migrainelike conditions are the result of a one-sided stuffing of material that must be learned without pleasure. The children are then filled with tiny spikes that do not get dissolved. They tend toward developing such spikes. Yes—we must be aware of these problems.

Second, immediately connected with the metabolic problems arising from boredom is the unhappy situation that does not allow us enough time for everything we ought to do. We should really see to it that the currently available readers—

which can drive you up the wall—are not used. The books I have seen in the classrooms are really quite awful.

We must not forget that we are preparing the children's physical constitutions for the rest of their lives. If we make them read the trivial stuff contained in most readers we affect their delicate organs accordingly. The children will turn into philistines rather than into complete human beings. We must know that the reading material we give our children strongly affects their development. The results are unavoidable in later life.

I really would like to ask you to compile your own anthologies, including the classics and other worthwhile authors, and to refrain from using the available books. This additional effort is necessary. We must do something. It is, after all, the task of the Waldorf school to use methods different from those practiced elsewhere. What matters is that in reading or storytelling, and also in the presentation of the natural sciences, we take great care not to harm the children in these two ways.

Eurythmy and singing lessons can be said to be working in the opposite direction, engendering an organic process that is quite different. All the organs connected with these activities contain spirit. When the children are doing eurythmy they move, and during the moving the spirit in the limbs is streaming upward. When we ask the children to do eurythmy or to sing, we liberate the spirit. The spiritual, of which the limbs abound, is liberated—a very real process. In our singing and eurythmy lessons we release the spiritual from the children. As a consequence, the released or liberated spirit expects to be made use of after these exercises. I explained this to you in yesterday's lecture in another connection. The spirit now also waits to be consolidated.

In singing, eurythmy, and physical education we spiritualize the children. They are quite different beings at the end of the lesson; there is much more spirit in them. But this spirit wishes to consolidate, wishes to remain with the children. We must not allow it to dissipate. We can prevent it from dissipating quite simply and effectively by making the children sit or stand quietly at the end of the lesson. We should try to maintain this calm for a few minutes. The older the children, the more important this will be. We should pay attention to these things if we wish to prepare the children in the best possible way for the following day. It is not in the children's interest for us to let them rush out of the room immediately after a gym, singing, or eurythmy lesson. We should, instead, let them calm down and sit quietly for a few minutes.

In considering such matters we really touch on a cosmic principle. There are many and diverse theories about matter and spirit. But both, matter and spirit, contain something that is more than either of them, a higher element. We may say that if this higher element is brought to a state of calm, it is matter; if it is brought into movement, it is spirit. This being a high principle, we can apply it to the human being. Through the short period of calm following a gym, singing, or eurythmy lesson or other such activity, we produce in ourselves—for the spirit we have liberated—a delicate physical phantom, which then deposits itself in our organism for us to make use of. Knowing about this process can help us make discoveries that will have corresponding effects in our other interactions with the children.

We shall now consider further uses for this knowledge. There are children in our school with a very vivid imagination, and there are children with very little imagination. We need not jump to the conclusion that half of our students are poets and the other half not. We notice the difference not so much in the actual way the imagination shows itself but rather in the way memory develops. Memory is strongly related to imagination. We have some children—and we should notice them—who quickly forget what they have experienced and heard during a lesson, who cannot hold on to the pictures of what they have experienced, for whom the pictures disappear. And we have other children for whom the pictures remain, assume an independent life of their own, and surface continuously, cannot be controlled. We should be well aware of these two types of children. There is, of course, a whole range between these extremes. For children with a vivid imagination, memory causes the pictures to surface in a changed form. Most frequently, however, the pictures surface unchanged, as reminiscences. The children are then slaves to what they have experienced during their lessons. And then there are the children for whom everything disappears, evaporates.

It is now a matter of dealing with these two types of children appropriately. It is possible to occupy groups of children in the most diverse ways if we develop a routine in the best sense of the word—a routine in a spiritual sense. Children with poor memory, who have difficulty in getting the pictures to surface, should be made to observe better during reading. We should try to get them to listen better. With children who are slaves to their mental pictures, we should see to it that they become more physically active, mobile; we should make them concentrate more on writing. We could have two groups in the class—giving the children who are poor in imagination the opportunity for cultivating their reading and observation, while for the other group, the children with a vivid imagination, we could especially cultivate painting and writing. Naturally, it is a matter of degree, because everything is relative.

We can take this distinction further. (But the following observation is especially important: We can only gradually learn these things; we cannot cover everything during the first year.) Children who are poor in imagination—that is, children who cannot easily remember—should be asked to do eurythmy standing up, mainly with their arms. Children with a vivid imagination who are tormented by their mental pictures will benefit by moving the whole body, be it by running or by walking. This we can encourage. It really is very important that we pay attention to such matters.

In addition, we ought to know the value of the consonants for phlegmatic children who find it difficult to recall mental pictures, whereas the children who are tormented by their ever-surfacing mental pictures will greatly benefit from eurythmy exercises that concentrate mainly on vowel sounds. It can indeed be observed that vowel exercises have a calming effect on the rising mental pictures, while consonant exercises engender them. Acting on this knowledge can help both groups.

The same distinction applies to music lessons. Children poor in imagination and memory should be encouraged to play musical instruments; children with a vivid imagination should be occupied with singing. It would be ideal—if we had the necessary rooms—to teach both groups simultaneously, one in singing, the other in instrumental music. If we could practice a twofold method—listening to *and* making music—this would have a tremendously harmonizing effect on the children. It would be most valuable if we could make it possible to alternate between singing and listening: to let half the class sing and the other half listen, and then vice versa. This practice should really be cultivated, because listening to music has a hygienic, a healing effect on what the head is to do in the human organism; singing has a healing effect on what the body is to do in the head. If we carried out everything that we could in this way, we would have far healthier people about.

We are not really aware of the fact that we have regressed in human evolution. In the past, children were allowed to grow up without being educated; their freedom was not invaded. Now we violate this freedom when we begin to educate them in the sixth or seventh year. We must make up for this crime, this destruction of freedom, by educating them correctly. We must be quite clear that it is the manner of education, the "how," that we have to improve if we wish to avoid a terrible future situation. It does not matter how much today people insist on stressing the cultural progress, the dwindling number of illiterates—they themselves are no more than imprints, the automata made by the schools. We must avoid this end, must not produce mere imprints in our schools. We must allow our children to develop in their individuality.

This issue becomes especially important when we make use of artificial methods such as learning by rote or by heart. In repeating something in this way the children transmit the content of what they have learned from the soul and spirit to the physical organism. What is learned by heart must first be understood. But during the process of learning by heart the children gradually slither into an ever more mechanical, physical way of learning. This is the way along which the content of learning is taken—from the initial subjective element to the objective element.

We must be honest in such matters. When the content is taken to the objective level, we must make the children listen to themselves, must make them aware that they are hearing themselves speak. We must bring the children to the point that, to the same extent as they recite the lines, they listen to themselves. We can succeed in this if, for example, the children differentiate the sounds they produce. We tell them: "What you are speaking is all about you, and you can hear it." We must try to get the children to the point that they can hear themselves speak.

But this is not enough. Something else is even more important. We shall never succeed in letting the children find the transition from having the content of the words in their thoughts and feelings to learning it by heart if we do not appeal most strongly to their feelings before the memorizing begins.

The children must never be asked to learn anything by heart before they have a deep feeling for all the details contained in the words—especially a feeling that allows them to relate to the content in the right way.

Let us consider an extreme case. Let us think of a prayer. The children should, when asked to learn a prayer, be urged to be in a mood of devotion. It is up to us to see to this. We must almost feel a horror if we teach the children a prayer without first establishing this mood of reverence or devotion. And they should never say a prayer without this mood. We should thus not make the children recite a lovely poem without first arousing in them a faint smile, a pleasure or joy; we should not order them to have these feelings but rather allow the content of the poem to awaken them. This principle applies to other subjects as well.

Much harm has been done to humankind during the course of evolution. Certainly, things have improved a little in this respect. But my generation remembers the way children were made to memorize, for example, historical dates and other facts. I myself remember history lessons during which teacher and children read a paragraph in a textbook and the children were afterward supposed to remember it; they simply learned it by heart. I heard an intelligent boy speak of the "Car of Jerusalem" instead of the "Czar of Russia"! He did not notice the gaffe during his mechanical recital of a passage in the book. This is not an isolated case. This method of learning things by heart in such subjects as geography and history has greatly contributed to our present cultural decadence.

It is essential to prepare the children correctly for such things that are to be learned by heart: prayers and poems. Their feelings must be engendered, the feelings they must have when they listen to themselves. Especially during the saying of a prayer, the children must have the feeling: "I grow above myself. I am saying something that makes me grow above myself." This mood must apply to everything that is beautiful and graceful.

The mood also affects the physical organism, has a hygienic significance, because every time we teach something of a tragic or exalted nature we affect the metabolism. Every time we teach something of a graceful, dainty nature we affect the head, the nerve-sense organism. We can thus proceed in a hygienic way. Children who are flippant, lightheaded, who are always bent on sensations, we shall try to cure by producing in them the mood they must have for something of a sublime, tragic nature. This will already be beneficial. We must pay attention to such matters in our lessons.

You will be able to do this if you yourselves have the right attitude to your teaching. Every now and then, in an almost meditative way, you ought to answer the question: How does my teaching of history or geography affect the children? It is necessary for us as teachers to know what we are doing. We have spoken about the way history and geography ought to be taught, but it is not enough to know it; it must be recalled in brief meditations. Does the teacher of eurythmy, for example, know that he releases the spirit from the children's limbs? Does the teacher, during a reading lesson, know that she incorporates the spirit in the children?

If the teacher becomes aware of these things, she will almost see that when she is reading in the wrong way, when she bores the children, they will tend toward metabolic illness; she will feel that by making a child read a boring piece of literature, she actually produces a diabetic in later life. She will then develop the right sense of responsibility. By occupying the children continuously with boring material, you produce diabetics. If you don't calm the released spirit after a physical exercise or a singing lesson, you produce people who lose themselves in life.

It is extraordinarily important that teachers thus occasionally reflect on what they are doing. But the reflection need not be oppressive. The teacher who is primarily concerned with reading will through it develop the feeling that she is actually continuously incorporating something, that she is working at the physical organism, and that she makes the children, through the way they are reading, into physically strong or weak adults. The teacher of handwork or crafts will be able to say to himself that he affects especially the spiritual in the children. If we let the children do things in handwork or crafts that are meaningful, we shall do more for the spirit than if we let them do things that are generally believed to be spiritual.

Much can be done in this direction, because much of what the children are doing nowadays in handwork is quite wrong. We can work in a more positive way that will have especially good results. I immediately noticed the children in Dornach making pillows, little cushions, which they then embroidered. If the embroidery is merely arbitrary, it isn't really a cushion. The embroidery must be such that it invites the ear to lie on the cushion. The children seemed to especially enjoy making tea cosies. But they must be made properly. If I am to open the cosy at the bottom, the movement of my hands must be continued in the embroidery; the embroidery must indicate the opening of the cosy. But the children have been so ruined by the conditions of our time that they embroider the bottom of their cosies like this:

This is the wrong way round. The drawing must show where the opening is. When embroidering the top of a blouse or shirt, the children must learn that the embroidered band at the throat must widen toward the bottom and narrow toward the top. An embroidery on a belt must immediately show that it opens to both sides simultaneously; it must be widest at the center. Everywhere the children should learn to find the correct form.

Very much can be achieved by these things if we do not so much bother about the eye, but produce them in the feeling. You must get the children to feel what their design indicates: it widens at the bottom, it presses down from above. This must be translated into feeling; we must get, what the hands are supposed to do, into the hands. The human being is here essentially fully occupied in his whole being, thinks with his whole body. We really must try to see to it that such things are felt. The handwork lessons must be directed to feeling. The child should, when embroidering a corner, have the feeling: this corner must be embroidered in such a way that, when I put my finger into it, it can't get through. If it happens to be something else, the embroidery must indicate this. This is the way we ought to teach. The handwork teacher can then say: I teach in a way that I especially engender the children's spiritual activity. No teacher needs to feel that he or she occupies an inferior position in the school.

5

STUTTGART / JUNE 16, 1921

Today we shall take a look at the characteristic features of the fourteen- and fifteen-year-old children and then, during the following days, concentrate more on the corresponding practical educational aspects. And we shall consider the impact the education of this age group has on the whole school.

We know from our anthroposophical studies that the astral body is actually born at this age—that it comes into its own at this time. Just as the physical body is especially active from birth to the seventh year, and the etheric body from the seventh to the fourteenth or fifteenth year, the astral body (strongly connected with the ego) is active from the fourteenth to the twentieth or twenty-first year, when the ego can be said to be born.

The fourteenth and fifteenth years are especially important in child development. You can see this importance in the looser connection between the astral body and the etheric and physical bodies. Every night, during sleep, we leave our physical and etheric bodies with our astral body and ego. On the one side, our physical and etheric bodies are then closely linked; on the other side, we have a close connection between astral body and ego. Because of this alternating separation and rejoining, there is a looser connection, on the one hand, between the astral and etheric bodies and, on the other hand, between the ego and the physical body.

The transition for the human being at age fourteen or fifteen (earlier for girls) is different from the transition that takes place at seven years. At the change of teeth, when the children are ready for the elementary school, we have a situation that arises, as it were, quite objectively in the physical/corporeal outer nature of the human being, in that part that separates every day during sleep—an objective happening. During the transition at sexual maturity, the adolescent now relates his or her subjective life—the ego and the astral body—to the objective sphere, to the etheric and physical bodies. In this transition, the inner (soul) life is affected quite differently than it is during the transition at the change of teeth. During the earlier transition, a physical/etheric connection takes place—which affects the subjective life. During the transition at puberty, the physical and etheric bodies remain as they are, and the astral body and ego remain as they are, but there is now, in a certain sense, a different interaction between the two pairs. The physical/corporeal and the etheric bodies, on the one hand, and the astral body and the ego, on the other hand, participate in this transition with equal strength: The inner subjective qualities of the human being participate directly in this process.

The nature of this process accounts for the dramatic changes in character after puberty. The changes can be seen outwardly in a matured capacity for love, which does not immediately show itself in its full sexual form but does show itself, in a general way, in the more intimate, inner relationships in which the children attract each other. Friendships are formed between girls and boys in which the sexual aspects do not initially play a role; rather, the friendships show the beginning of a more conscious development of the forces of love, of the forces needed for relating to and caring for another being at this new stage in development.

We can then see, beginning at puberty, in the outer behavior of both girls and boys, something that often baffles their parents and teachers, something that contradicts their previous character: the teenagers' loutish behavior (especially in boys, differently in girls). This behavior is caused by the feelings of the astral body (which encloses the not yet fully developed ego) as it struggles to experience a right relation to the physical body and, through it, to the whole of the environment. Because of the need to discover a relation between the objective and the subjective, this inner struggle is unavoidable. It expresses itself in a denial, as it were, of what the adolescent has so far developed. We sometimes do not recognize the teenagers—they are so different from what they used to be.

I need not go into detailed descriptions; we are all familiar with teenage behavior. But we must understand its nature, because of its significance for education.

What we see initially is that the astral body has a stronger influence in girls than in boys. Throughout life the astral body of women plays a more important role than that of men. The whole of the female organism is organized toward the cosmos through the astral body. Much of what are really cosmic mysteries is unveiled and revealed through the female constitution. The female astral body is more differentiated, essentially more richly structured, than that of the male. Men's astral bodies are less differentiated, less finely structured, coarser.

Girls between the ages of thirteen or fourteen and twenty or twenty-one develop in such a way that their egos are strongly influenced by what goes on in their astral bodies. We can see how the ego of a girl is, one could say, gradually absorbed by the astral body, with the result that during her twentieth and twenty-first years there is a strong counterpressure, a strong effort to come to grips with the ego.

The process is essentially different in boys. Their astral bodies do not absorb their egos so strongly. Their egos are more concealed, are not as effective. The ego of the boy between the ages of thirteen or fourteen and twenty or twenty-one remains without the strong influence of the astral body. Because of this, because the ego of the boy is not absorbed by the astral body and yet lacks independence, boys at this age are less forward than girls. Girls are freer at this age, more at ease in their outer confrontation with the world than are boys. We can notice in those boys especially endowed with these qualities a reserve, a withdrawal from life, the result of this special relation between astral body and ego.

Certainly, boys are looking for friendship, for some connection. But they also feel the need to hide their thoughts and feelings. This is characteristic of boys whose egos are connected to their astral bodies in this way. Teachers who can empathize with this situation that is present in boys, who can meet it in a subtle, delicate way, will do much to help them. It is this manner of the teacher rather than a direct, crude approach that has a beneficial effect. The boy has a certain love of withdrawal into himself; if this love of withdrawing into himself is not present at this age in a boy we really ought to be cautious. A good teacher will notice this, and he or she will then take care. The teacher will reflect: "There is something I have to look for, something that isn't quite right, something that could cause problems and abnormalities in later life."

It is different with girls. With girls, there are delicate differences, for which it is necessary to develop a certain skill in observation. The girl's ego is more or less absorbed by the astrality. Because of this, the girl lives less strongly in her inner being. She takes her ego-permeated astral body into her etheric body. Her etheric body—that is, her behavior, her outer mobility—is strongly affected. We can observe in real girls—that is, in girls whose egos are absorbed by their astral bodies, who develop in a healthy, correct way—a courageous, firm demeanor during this time. They accentuate their personalities, are self-assured, do not withdraw into themselves. It is natural for them to confront the world freely and unashamedly.

If this demeanor is accompanied by even faint egotistical feelings, it can express itself in showing off, in a wish to display character and personality. But it is characteristic for girls during this time to wish to confront the world in this free uninhibited way and to show their worth. Taken to an extreme, this wish can lead to coquetry and vanity, not only to the display of inner (soul) life but also to self-adornment with jewelry. It is extraordinarily interesting to observe how what later leads to an addiction to makeup and a trivial love of finery can show itself as a delicate aesthetic sense during this time. All this is certainly the outward expression of the special relation of the ego-permeated astral body to the etheric body: The girls walk differently, their posture changes, they hold their heads more freely. Again, taken to an extreme, they become supercilious, and so on. We should indeed observe these things artistically.

If we bear in mind these differences between boys and girls we shall understand that the blessing of coeducation allows us to achieve much by a tactful treatment of both sexes in the same room. A conscientious teacher who is aware of his or her tasks in approaching such a coeducational situation will still differentiate between girls and boys. We must thus also differentiate with regard to what is so important at this age, what I just now characterized—namely, the way the subjective element has developed in its relation to the outer world. At this age, we are to relate the subjective element to our own body, to the etheric and physical bodies. The condition for doing so is one's relation to the outer world as such.

This can be prepared during the whole of elementary education. It is the task of every teacher; it concerns every teacher. We must, in our lessons, see to it that the children experience the beautiful, artistic, and aesthetic conception of the world; and their ideas and mental pictures should be permeated by a religious / moral feeling. Such feelings, when they are cultivated throughout the elementary school years, will make all the difference during the thirteenth, fourteenth, and fifteenth years. For a child whose feelings for the beautiful, for the aesthetic conception of the world, have not been stimulated will during puberty easily become overly sensual, even perhaps erotic. There is no better way of counteracting the erotic feelings than through the healthy development of the aesthetic sense for the sublime and beautiful in nature. If you succeed in making the children feel deeply the beauty, the colors, in sunrise and sunset, in the flowers, experience the sublime splendor of a thunderstorm—if, as it were, you cultivate in them the aesthetic sense—you will do more for them than is done by the often absurdly practiced sex education given to children at an ever younger age. It is the feeling for the beautiful, an aesthetic confrontation with the world, that counteracts the erotic feeling. By experiencing the world as beautiful, the human being will also attain the right, healthy relation to his or her body, will not be tormented by it, as happens in eroticism.

It is most important during puberty that the children have developed certain moral, religious feelings. Such feelings also strengthen the astral body and ego. They become weak if the religious, moral feelings and impulses have been neglected. The children then turn indolent, as though physically paralyzed. This will show itself especially during the years we are now discussing. The lack of moral and ethical impulses also leads to irregularities in the sexual life.

We must consider the differences between girls and boys in our education leading up to this age. We must make the effort to develop the girls' moral and ethical feelings in a way that they are directed toward the aesthetic life. We must take special care that the girls especially enjoy the moral, the religious, and the good in what they hear in the lessons. They should take pleasure in the knowledge that the world is permeated by the supersensible;

they should be given pictures that are rich in imagination, that express the world as permeated by the divine, that show the beautiful aspects of the good and moral human being.

In regard to boys, it will be necessary to provide them with ideas and mental pictures that tend toward strength and affect the religious and ethical life. With girls, we should bring the religious and moral life to their very eyes, while with boys we should bring the religious and beautiful predominantly into the heart, the mind, stressing the feeling of strength that radiates from them. Naturally, we must not take these things to an extreme, should not think of making the girls into aesthetic kittens that regard everything merely aesthetically. Nor should the boys be made into mere louts, as would be the inevitable result of their egotisms being engendered through an unduly strong feeling of their strength—which we ought to awaken, but only by connecting it to the good, the beautiful, and the religious.

We must prevent the girls from becoming superficial, from becoming unhealthy, sentimental connoisseurs of beauty during their teenage years. And we must prevent the boys from turning into hooligans. These dangers do exist. We must know the reality of these tendencies and must, during the whole of elementary education, see to it that the girls are directed to experience pleasure in the beautiful, to be impressed by the religious and aesthetic aspects of the lessons; and we must see to it that the boys are told: "If you do this, your muscles will grow taut, you will become a strong, efficient young man!" The sense of being permeated by the divine must really be kindled in boys in this way.

These now emerging special qualities are indeed founded—very delicately—in human nature. With regard to girls, the ego is absorbed in the astral body. This, of course, expresses the situation in a radical and extreme way, but doing so will help you to have a picture of it. There is something in this spiritual/soul process that is akin to physical blushing. The whole development during this time is really a blushing of spirit and soul. The ego's invasion of the astral body is a kind of blushing.

The situation is different in boys. The boy's ego is less mobile, does not absorb itself; we are dealing with a spirit and soul growing pale. This situation is easily noticed, is always present. The physical aspects must not deceive us here. When a girl is chlorotic (maid-pale), the condition fully corresponds to the blushing of spirit and soul. When a boy turns into a real lout who easily gets excited, this behavior does not contradict the fact that his soul and spirit are growing pale.

This is basically the expression of a new experience or feeling that takes hold of the whole being: the feeling of shame or embarrassment. It permeates the whole being and consists of the feeling: "I must have something in my individual, inner life that is mine, that I do not wish to share with anyone else; I must have secrets." This is the nature of shame or embarrassment. And this feeling reaches every part of the spiritual life and the soul, as far as the most unconscious regions.

If, as teachers and educators, we can feel this development, if we can respect this in our own inner life, and if we then walk past a girl or boy with this delicate feeling in us, a feeling that respects this inwardly reposing feeling of shame—this will already have an effect. There is no need for words. When we move among a group of children with the feeling that there is something in them they wish to conceal, to preserve—like an unopened flower—then the unspoken effect of one person on another will be soon noticed. To live with just such a feeling will already have a tremendous educational effect.

It is a strange fact that in spite of the children's outer manifestations and behavior, everything they do is nothing other than a modified feeling of shame or embarrassment. A girl who blushes in soul and spirit, has an air of confidence, shows herself to the world, confronts it unabashedly. It is peculiar to human nature that the outer manifestation contradicts the inner disposition during this time—this unabashed bearing, this bold confrontation with the world, this rebellious nature, this demand: "I will be treated fairly!" Anyone familiar with girls' boarding schools can tell you this. They don't accept unfair treatment; they insist on being treated fairly. They can now confront a teacher, will show her or him what's what. "We shall not be made use of!" All this is basically nothing other than—let me say—the other side of what reposes quite unconsciously deep down in their soul life as a kind of feeling of shame.

And the boys: The loutish behavior at first, then their rudeness and churlishness during the later teenage years are really nothing other than their reluctance to show the world what they actually are. Wishing to make contact, they move clumsily, lounge about, behave differently from what they actually are. This we ought to consider—boys at this age, due to their special constitution, behave differently from what they really are. They copy other people. While the child during the first seven years imitates naturally, the teenager does so consciously. He imitates somebody in his walk, in his speech, in his rudeness, makes an effort to copy a gentleman. All this expresses his wish to make contact with the world outside—a special characteristic of teenagers. It is basically the embarrassment of revealing their own being, the withdrawal into themselves, the pretense of being different from what they really are.

The worst thing a teacher can do at this time is to confront teenage boys without humor. The proper humor consists in showing an interest in what they are up to, yet making it clear to them that you, the teacher, do not take it too seriously. You ought to develop these two ways of dealing with the situation. If you allow yourselves to be nettled by the boys' behavior, if you get into a rage, you will lose their respect. If you behave like the teacher who reacted to the boorish behavior of the boys by starting to shout: "If you don't shut up, I'll throw the duster at you!"—the children will no longer respect you.

A different method applies to the girls. The teacher ought to react to their coquetry with a certain delicate grace and then, speaking metaphorically, turn away: gracefully to pay attention, as it were, to what they are doing and, at the same time not to let them notice that one is affected by it. We allow them to exhaust their rage, especially the saucy, impertinent ones. We then leave them to themselves. With the boys, we empathize more with their loutish, rude behavior, at the same time showing them that we don't take it all too seriously, that we laugh a little, but not too much, so that they do not need to be cross.

What matters is that we develop a feeling for meeting the children's needs at this age and that we realize that each child is different. The outer manifestations are those of a metamorphosed feeling of shame or embarrassment that permeates the whole being. We prepare—and we must do so—the children correctly for their life in their twenties by recognizing the fact that the subjective element connects with the astral body in an independent way. Just as the human body needs a solid bone system to prevent it from sagging, so does the astral body, with its enclosed ego, need ideals at this age if it is to develop in a healthy way. We must take this seriously. Ideals, strong concepts that are permeated with will, these we must impart into the astral body as a firm, solid support.

We can notice that boys especially feel a strong need at this age—we only have to discover this and understand it correctly—for: "Everybody must choose his own hero, whom he has to follow on his way to Mt. Olympus." And it is especially important for us to present to the boys a fine ideal, a picturesque personality, be it a mythical character or a merely imaginative one, and to elaborate it, together with the boys, or to provide the elements for such elaboration. During a field trip we could have a conversation with the one or another of the boys, entering his particular needs. We could say to him: "How would you do this or that?" We point to the future, introduce the idea of purpose, of the aims in life. We, as it were, stiffen the astral body, make it firm—and this is important at this age.

The same applies to girls. If we make use of this knowledge, we shall also educate the girls correctly by recognizing the fact that they are more inclined to the cosmos and boys more inclined to the earth. Girls incline more toward the cosmic, and this means that their ideals are heroes and heroines; we should tell the girls about them, about their lives and deeds, about actual experiences. Boys need to hear about character, about complete human beings. This is essential; we must differentiate the needs of girls and boys.

It is important during this age to introduce to the students the world outside, so that they come to grips with and understand life as such. It is especially important for us to know this at the time when we are adding the tenth grade class to our school. Our lessons must be directed to the point at which the subjective may connect with the objective. And this is certainly not possible if we limit ourselves to the curricula currently practiced in the conventional high schools—because their curricula are the result of the influence of the intellectual world conception. You see, this merely formalistic way of educating our high school students, this one-sidedly cognitive, intellectual approach, this is something we should not continue with in our curriculum. And in not continuing this approach we shall not sin against progress in civilization.

Our curriculum should be such that it allows the children to become practical in life; it should connect them with the world. Our curriculum for the tenth grade class will, therefore, be based on the following: We must, in order to do justice to the social life, have girls and boys together in the room; but we must differentiate by giving them activities suited to their sex. We must not separate them. The boys should watch the girls during their activities and vice versa. There should be a social communication. We should also include the process that takes the thoughts from the head into the movements of the hand, even if this happens to be merely learned or theoretical. It must, as it were, be then a theory of the practical. It is, therefore, necessary to give the boys something that is appropriate for this age: lessons in mechanics—not only theory, as in physics, but practical mechanics, leading to the making of machines. Our curriculum for the tenth grade class must include the basic elements of practical mechanics.

In regard to the girls, we must provide them with something that allows them to have clear ideas of the skills involved in spinning and weaving. Girls must learn to understand the processes in spinning and weaving, must learn how spun and woven material is produced; they must learn to recognize a material that was mechanically produced, must be introduced to the mechanical processes and learn to relate to them. This belongs to this age group.

The boys, on the other hand, must, even if only in an elementary way that allows them to understand it, be taught the principles of surveying and mapping a pasture or forest. This is again essential for this age. Girls must learn the basic elements of hygiene and first aid, the different ways of bandaging.

Both sexes must participate in all these activities. Spinning, weaving, hygiene, and first aid are taught to the girls; the boys will do this later. And the girls must observe the boys handling the surveyance instruments. We can do this in the Waldorf School, can get the boys to draw a precise map of a certain area.

In short, we shall awaken in our students an understanding of what must be done in life if it is to go on. Without such an understanding, we continue to live in a foreign environment.

This, in fact, is the terrible characteristic of our time—that people are living in an environment that is foreign to them. You only have to walk into the street and take a good look at the people boarding a street car or bus. How many of them actually know how this street car is set in motion, know about the natural forces necessary for it? This has an effect on the whole human constitution—spirit, soul, and body. There is a great difference between having at least an elementary knowledge of the things we use in daily life and not having such knowledge. Traveling in a car, plane, or bus, using an electrical gadget without understanding at least the underlying principles, means blindness of soul and spirit. Just as a blind person is moving through life without experiencing the effects of light, so do people move blindly through the cultural life, because they cannot see, did not have the opportunity to learn to see and understand, the objects around them. This is a defect of spirit and soul. And the damages we see in our advanced civilizations are the result of people's blindness in regard to their environment.

There is something else we have to consider: There is a great difference between learning something before and learning something after the age of nineteen or twenty. People generally learn a trade like surveying at nineteen or later. High school education, especially in grammar schools, does not include such practical subjects. But the long-term effect depends on it. What we learn after the nineteenth year impresses itself more outwardly; what we learn and experience at fifteen permeates our whole being, becomes as one with the human spirit, so that it is not merely a job we can manage, but a job we can identify with, in which our entire being participates. This applies also to the elementary aspects of mechanics, engineering, and the subjects I mentioned in regard to the education of girls.

We must insist on cultivating in our students such feelings and inner qualities that can then live and grow as their limbs are growing. Human development does not proceed by fixing two arms to the body—during the third seven-year period—two arms that then remain the way they are; they must continue to grow. Today's endeavors are such that the students are instructed in a way that what they are learning cannot continue to live but remains unchanged throughout life. The things we learn must continue to live in us. This is only possible if they are learned at the right age. And we have to admit that somebody whose specific skills direct him or her to a certain occupation and who then bases his training on something he already knows—this building on something one already knows will have a tremendous significance for the whole of life.

I have always valued the lectures given by the anatomist Hyrtl. His subject was descriptive and topographical anatomy. Hyrtl belonged to the older generation. He demanded that his students read the relevant chapters in his excellent books prior to the lectures, and he emphasized the fact that he did not wish to lecture on a subject the students had not previously read about. He did this with so much charm that he managed to make his students see the value of this method, and even the lazier ones among them conformed to his wishes—a remarkable achievement, as most of you will appreciate.

Translator's note: The difference between students is today no longer understood as necessarily sexually determined—as a difference between boys and girls. Some boys tend to a female astral/ego constitution, and some girls to a male astral/ego constitution. In most Waldorf schools the students may decide which practical subjects they wish to take. The principle remains: doing activities and observing the other students' activities.

6

STUTTGART / JUNE 17, 1921

As we consider the education of the older children, it will be especially necessary to address ourselves to the deeper aspects of human life and the cosmos. Without such a deeper understanding of life, we cannot really in good conscience accept the tasks connected with the high school.

We must understand that life is actually a totality, a oneness, and that by removing any one part of it, we do harm to it. As children, we grow into this life as we find it. We are placed into it by, in a way, sleeping into it. Just think of the absolutely unconscious way children confront the world during their first years. They then gradually increase their consciousness. But what does this mean? It means that the children learn to adapt their inner life to the world outside, to connect the outer world to the inner, the inner to the outer. They also learn to be conscious of the outer objects and to differentiate themselves from those objects.

This dichotomy between inner and outer grows ever stronger. The children look up, beyond the horizon, at the sky, they perceive the cosmos, they may even sense the existence of cosmic laws; but as a rule, the children grow into the totality of the world, into which they are received, without in any way getting close to the mystery of the connection between the human being and the cosmos.

The children continue to grow, they are cared for by the people around them, they are educated and instructed. The children develop in such a way that the necessity of participating in world events in some form or other rises from their whole individuality.

We prepare the children for world events by letting them play during the early years, thus awakening their activity. We make every effort to do things with them that meet and satisfy their needs, to educate them healthfully, hygienically—body, soul, and spirit. We try to do something else. We try to adapt them to the demands of the social and technological life. The attempt is made to educate the children in a way that allows them, later in life, to work, to participate in events, to interact with other people. We try to teach them skills and facts that allow them to participate in the technological life, so that their work can be meaningful and valuable for society, so that they themselves may find their place in life, their connection to the social life, to other people.

We do all of this. And in order that we do this in the right way, so that we, on the one hand, really meet the needs of human nature, so that we do not place human beings into the world with spiritually, psychologically (soul), and physically sick or stunted organisms, we must, on the other hand, admit to ourselves that human beings must grow into the social life in such a way that they can do something by which they may advance both themselves and the world. We must see to meeting both these demands.

And yet we have to tell ourselves that it is not easy today to accomplish this, to give the children what they need in these two areas. And if we take an unbiased look at our situation as teachers, it even causes us a certain skepticism, a certain doubt. We can easily understand today's concerns and the many discussions on the subject. How should our children be educated? What should we do?

All these questions and problems that arise in our culture with such vehemence did not exist in older civilizations. You only need to study these old cultures without bias. Of course, there were a lot of things in those cultures that are incomprehensible to us today. We quite justifiably reject the slave and helot system of ancient Greece. But when we study the Greeks' views on education, we shall soon see that such discussions as we have today—discussions in which so many diverse and opposing opinions are thrown about—would have been unthinkable then.

Beyond the effort we put into teaching, we need educational methods, and we need to develop teaching skills. But when we watch the heated discussions and see the impossibility of agreement—some emphasize the physical, some the mental-academic aspects, some these, some those methods—we arrive at the conclusion not only that teaching has become difficult but that in regard to our position as teachers and educators we cannot break away from being ignoramuses.

We should really have this feeling of helplessness; and it will, I believe, be even more pronounced if we take a wider view of the situation. You will get this wider view when you study how the current outpouring of educational principles and ideas has its roots in central European culture. I suggest that you make yourselves familiar with everything that was said about spiritual, psychological, and physical education by individuals steeped in central European cultural life. Read the books by Dittes and Diesterweg; read about their views on education.

I recommend to you the interesting essay in Karl Julius Schroer's book *Aspects of Education* [*Unterrichtsfragen*], in which—quite correctly, I believe—he speaks of the place of physical education in the curriculum and offers a detailed program for this subject. During your perusal, I would like for you to consider the mode of thinking and the attitudes from which the thoughts arise. Consider how despite the real understanding of physical human nature and of the need to prepare the children for becoming practical and efficient adults, there is nonetheless also a strong consciousness of the reality of the soul and of the necessity to consider the human soul in all aspects of education.

Then compare—not the outward features; as anthroposophists you ought to be above doing that—compare what lies embedded in the depths of the soul, compare the basic attitudes contained in any of the numerous treatises on education in the Anglo-American literature. Everywhere in this literature you will find chapters on intellectual, aesthetic, and physical education. Think of the deeply held conviction from which they are written. You will get the feeling that the word "education" no longer applies. Everywhere in this culture—even when spiritual or intellectual education is mentioned—the human being is thought of as a kind of mechanism; it is thought that if the physical/corporeal organism, or mechanism, is properly developed, all the moral and intellectual development will follow as though by itself. We have with this view a much stronger inclination to the physical/corporeal in the human being.

I would like to suggest that the central European writers assume that it is possible to include soul and spirit in education and that by doing this the correct treatment of the physical will follow. The Anglo-Saxon idea emphasizes physical education. One then ignores a kind of tiny room inside the human being; one "educates" around the physical, along the periphery, and assumes that there is a tiny room in which the intellect and the moral and religious life are locked up, a kind of instinctive and logical religious and moral life. Once the physical body has been sufficiently educated, its forces will spread to within and dissolve the walls of this room, and the intellectual, moral, and religious life will by itself rush out. We must learn to read between the lines when we study these books and thus discover the underlying reasons and attitudes.

It is necessary to pay attention to these differentiations across the world today. It is much more important than merely observing superficially, in the modern fashion, when one considers these symptoms. Try to understand these symptoms of our transitional culture by following the extraordinarily important debates that have taken place in England during recent weeks. The debates have been triggered by the worsening social conditions and by the general industrial actions (strikes) that have threatened the whole social life. The press was reporting these discussions in full. And then, suddenly, a complete change of interest. Why? A season of ball games has begun, and interest in sport overshadows the interest in the most important social matters. Those involved in the discussions try to get away from the debating rooms as quickly as possible, rushing to the tennis courts, the football fields, and so on, with the feeling: "I want to move in a way that my muscles can grow as strongly as possible; I am interested in such important things." I am probably describing the feeling in an amateurish way, but I cannot be bothered about detailed facts in this cultural phenomenon: "I am interested in such important matters as watching how somebody throws a ball-like object and how somebody else can catch it correctly with his big toe or another part of his body."

The picture we get from studying these differentiations is indeed a peculiar one. Reading the papers is of little use. What the journalists are writing is of little significance. It is far more important to discover their reasons for writing about a subject. To enter a discussion with people, to listen to their opinions, is quite useless today. It is far more profitable to discover what is living deep down in their souls, to discover what induces them to act in a certain way, to have this or that opinion. It is this that matters today. What the French and German ministers are saying to each other, if one agrees with either the one or the other, is of no importance whatsoever. It cannot be the concern of someone who wishes to participate in the progress of our civilization. What matters is to discover the differing nature of the untruths expressed by these individuals. We must keep in mind the intentions behind the lies of both speakers.

We must know that we are living at a time when the words people are speaking have no longer any meaning; the forces behind and between the words are significant. A teacher wishing to educate modern youths must understand this, must become part of his or her age in this way, must do so in an ever deeper sense. But the teacher must not share the current basic characteristic attitudes and mode of thinking. When we today—permeated even a little with anthroposophical consciousness—take a walk in the streets, we no longer see human people; rather we see moles that move about in the smallest of circles, circles into which they were placed, moles whose thinking is limited to these narrow circles, cannot reach beyond them, moles who take no interest in what is happening outside these circles. If we do not succeed in growing beyond this molelike existence, if we cannot do more than reproduce the judgments and opinions—from various points of view—to which we have been conditioned through the events at the end of the nineteenth century and the beginning of the twentieth century, then we cannot positively participate in what ought to be done, in order to overcome this unhappy situation.

If there is anyone who ought to be gripped by what I have just outlined, it is the teacher in charge of the young, who wishes especially to help the students to come to terms with their more mature age in the ninth and tenth grade classes. The whole school must be so structured that such ideas can be included. To do this, it is necessary to understand them even better, so that all of us, not only those directly involved in the higher classes, but all the teachers, can say to ourselves that what matters is that we have an elementary feeling for the whole of education and its practical application, that we experience the whole weight and force of our task—to place human beings into the world. Without this experience of our task, our Waldorf School will be no more than a phrase. We shall say all sorts of beautiful things about it, until the holes have become so large that we shall lose the ground under our feet. We must make it inwardly true, and we can do this only by getting ourselves to the stage at which we can have a thorough understanding of the teaching profession.

As we do this, the question will surely arise: As human beings at the present time, what are we really? We were placed into our age through the way we were brought up, conditioned by the events during the last third of the nineteenth century and the beginning of the twentieth century. And what are you today, my dear friends? Some of you have studied philosophy or history in the way these subjects were taught in the high schools and universities at the beginning of this century. Some of you have studied mathematics or other practical subjects. Some of you have become teachers of singing or physical education. Various methods were used in teaching these subjects. There are those among you who, according to the predilection of the staff, accepted the model of the gentleman or lady, but with a physical/corporeal understanding. There are those of you who have preferred what could be called a more inward path, but a path made inward through intellectualism. We are the sum total, the result of the ways we were conditioned—as far as into our fingertips and toes.

We must be quite clear about our task today—namely, to take full charge of what has been implanted in us through our education. This is possible only through a timely exploration of conscience that extends beyond the individual aspects. Without such exploration we cannot grow beyond what our time can provide us with. And we must grow beyond what our time can give us. We must not become puppets of the trends developed at the end of the nineteenth century and the beginning of the twentieth century. Above all, we must admit to the limitations of what is given us by today's culture; through a comprehensive exploration of conscience, we must attain the correct knowledge, knowledge that will allow us to find our place in life.

At this point we ask: Has not everything that has made us the way we are been infected by the materialistic attitudes of our time? Certainly, there is no shortage of goodwill. But even this goodwill has been infected by the views that are the result of the natural-scientific world conception. And our knowledge of physical education has emerged from such views.

Humankind has really always wanted to hide from, to avoid, the necessity of exploring its conscience. Humankind has wanted to avoid the exploration that would thoroughly stir up its inner life by asking: How do we older people confront the young? When we look at the girls and boys reaching the age of sexual maturity, when we see them coming to us after having attained this maturity—if we wish to be honest with ourselves, we can only have one answer to the question: We don't know what we should do for them, unless we educate and teach on the basis of fundamentally new concepts. Otherwise, we produce nothing but a wide gap between the young and ourselves.

This great question has practical dimensions. Take a good look at the youth movements as they have developed today. They are nothing else but documentation that our various experimentations have resulted in the loss of our leadership in education. Just look at what has happened. At the age we are now discussing, the young feel inwardly urged to withdraw from the leadership of the old, to take their guidance into their own hands; this happened with tremendous rapidity. We cannot fault the young for this. Discussion of this phenomenon is of great spiritual-scientific interest but not initially of pedagogical interest. Our pedagogical interest must be limited to the fact that the old have been responsible for their loss of leadership and understanding of the young.

Since the old no longer have anything of substance to give to the young, the teenagers and adolescents have formed themselves into groups [*Wandervögel*] that traverse the countryside with singing and conversing, searching in a vague way for what the older generation has failed to provide. Thoughts and words have become hollow; the older generation having nothing to give to the young, the young then roam the woods, searching among themselves for what they cannot receive from the words and models of their elders. It is one of the most significant phenomena of the present time. The young find themselves confronted by the great question that used to be answered in the past by the older generation but that now can no longer be answered by them, because their language is no longer comprehensible.

Remember your own youth? You had, perhaps, more courage than the members of such groups, took less interest in traipsing through the countryside. You managed to survive somehow. You pretended to listen to the older generation and adhered to the status quo. But the *Wandervögel* do not pretend. They have withdrawn from the older generation and have taken to the woods. We have seen this happen, and we have also witnessed the results of this youth movement. Not so long ago, they felt the need to make contact among themselves, wishing to discover for themselves what they could not get from their teachers, wishing to escape them and take refuge in nature. They mean to find their answers in some vague, undefined sphere. They make contact among themselves, forming small cliques.

It really is a strange phenomenon that is immensely instructive. The old have lost their leadership, have become philistines. They cannot accept the fact that this deep longing has awakened in the young, in the members of such groups. And how have the old reacted to this, those among them who are at least a little affected by modern times? They do not say to themselves: "We must advance to a deep exploration of conscience; we must from our mature stage of development find a way to the young." No, they react differently: "Since the young," they say, "do no longer wish to learn from us, we shall learn from them." And you can see this happening in all our educational institutions—the old adapting to the will and demands of the young. When you look at this new phenomenon without prejudice, you will see that the old wish to be led by the young, that they have placed the leadership into their hands—representatives of the student body are now counselors and members of boards and trusts in educational institutions.

We must consider the deeper implications of this phase. What has it done to the young? They have passed from their need for contact, from their wish to find themselves in cliques, to searching for their inner (soul) life in a hermit existence. The final stage of this development is a kind of fear of contact, everyone feeling the necessity of relying only on himself or herself. The former certainty of finding answers in the world outside has given way to a kind of atomizing longing, a brooding: "What is the reason for my inability to do justice to the human being in me?" You can see this feeling spreading everywhere; you only need to be awake enough to see it. You can see this growing uncertainty in the fragmentation of soul forces. You can perceive a special fear, a *horror vacui,* that makes the young shudder and feel scared in view of their future. They are fearful of the life ahead of them. There is basically only one answer, one remedy—the deep exploration of conscience. And this cannot limit itself to externalities but must lead to the question: How has it come to pass that we, when we wish to lead and guide the young, no longer understand them with the forces of the old?

Let us, by contrast, take a look at a distant age, such as that of the ancient Greeks. The older Greeks, as we know from history, still had a certain understanding for the young. If you try to understand Greek culture, you will find a peculiar and very definite relation between the period from the thirteenth or fourteenth to the twentieth or twenty-first year and the period from the twenty-eighth to the thirty-fifth year. This is characteristic of both the Greek and Roman cultures—that people in their late thirties had a fine understanding for children between seven and fourteen and that people in their early thirties felt a special affinity for, an understanding for the needs of, teenagers and adolescents. There was this relation according to different age groups—a relation of those in the third seven-year period with those in the fifth and a relation of those in the second seven-year period with those in the sixth.

It really is not easy to see behind the mysteries of human evolution. But we can indeed clearly feel that for the Greeks when the girls and boys arrived at sexual maturity they looked up to the twenty-eight- and twenty-nine-year-olds, choosing the ones they liked best, the ones they wished to emulate in freedom. They could no longer obey an authority as such, only one of their choosing in this specific age group. As humanity evolved through the Middle Ages to our time, this relation became ever weaker until it disappeared altogether. People were thrown together in a helter-skelter way; a spiritually given structure gave way to chaos. This very real situation has, then, prompted a social problem in our world; in education, it has prompted a pedagogical/didactic problem. Without keeping in mind the whole of evolution, we cannot make any progress.

I would like to show you the cause for this phenomenon by pointing to a concrete fact. All you have then to do is to generalize this concrete fact in order to discover the causes for this lack of understanding between the old and the young. You see, during our current preparation for life, during our education, we are, for example, taught that there are some one hundred elements. We learn this, and when we become teachers we are, as a rule, aware of these chemical elements—that they exist, even though this theory has recently come under attack. But we have absorbed this knowledge, carry it within us, the knowledge that there are these one hundred or so elements, that through their synthesis and analysis everything in the world comes about. We even develop a world conception on this basis. And this is the farce, that during the last third of the nineteenth century a world conception was constructed on the basis of the then seventy chemical elements. This prompted the question: How could the planets, everything that solidified, arise through chemical and physical changes? How did abiogenesis come about through an especially complicated chemical synthesis? It was the wish to comprehend the whole world with thoughts that had their roots in such elements.

The Greeks would have thought of this one-sided intellectual (head) approach to the world as nonsense, as inhuman. If they had been told to imagine the world as the result of the synthesis and analysis of these one hundred elements, they would have felt, deep down, as though the human being would disintegrate into dust during the process. The Greeks would not have been able to comprehend it. What indeed would a human being do with such a world that consists of these elements that synthesize and analyze? What does it mean? What would happen? The world could well be there, be a gigantic cosmic test tube, but the human being, how would the human being exist in it? Is is as though we were to put a large test tube in a room, allow all sorts of elements to boil in it, and then open a door and push a human being through an opening into the tube, into this mixture of salts and acids. This the Greeks would have imagined if they had been asked to think of the world as structured by these elements. They would not have accepted this idea, their feelings would have resisted it. The picture I have just characterized would have arisen instinctively in their minds.

But we are not merely heads. It was only at fairgrounds that living, talking heads used to be shown as exhibits. No, we don't exist as head only but as complete human beings. And if we wish to develop such ideas with only the head, if our life of feeling, of will, and of the whole physical organism were to be so constituted that we could believe in a world made up of such stuff, we would have to feel very differently, would have something different in our fingertips than what the Greeks had, the Greeks who would have dismissed such a notion as pure nonsense. One feels differently about, places oneself differently into, a world if one believes that the world is something that is fit for a test tube but not for the universe. The same point applies with regard to the social life in ancient Greece. We must consider these things.

We don't just *think* that the world consists of one hundred elements. We carry this *feeling* into everything we do during the day—even when we wash and dry our hands. The fact that it is possible for our head to have such an inhuman world conception while we wash ourselves—thinking in this way impresses a definite quality into our feelings. And then—when we can think and feel in this way, when there is no room for the human being in such a world conception—when we then confront the fifteen-year-old girls and boys with this thinking and feeling, it should come as no surprise that we cannot reach them, that we don't know what to do with our feeling and thinking. With this world conception we can lecture in universities and colleges, teaching what we believe to be right, but we cannot live with it. The graduates of our universities then become teachers who have no idea of their connection with the young. This is the terrible abyss that has opened up before us.

But as far as human beings are concerned, there is something in us at the age of fifty or fifty-five that bears a certain resemblance to today's teaching of chemistry and physics. We then have become sclerosed to the extent that our inner organism faintly resembles the world outside. The cosmic powers are gradually doing something with us during the course of our lives on earth. We, too, harden in our physical organism in older age. At about fifty, we become dissociated; we, as it were, disintegrate inwardly into dust. But this dissolution is a gradual, slow process, not as cruel as what would be happening to us in a test tube. Neither does it go that far—although it has the same tendency; it is a more humane process. But at the age when we approach death something does begin to be active in us that is synonymous with the teaching of modern science. Our world conception is such that only the very old may comprehend it. Nature is kind. It compensates the old by making them childish.

Talking about such things in this way may make it seem as though one wishes to poke fun at the world. No, it is not a matter of humor; it is a matter of the deepest tragedy. It is true. We are describing the world today as processes that are synonymous with those in human corpses, no more. After our death something similar takes place. In older age, we have a presentiment of the processes in our physical body after death. And we describe nothing else in our modern sciences. Our cultural institutions are full with such knowledge that applies to the physical human being after death. But such knowledge does not live in our limbs. Such are the feelings we absorb from the thoughts given us today. And the traditional theological beliefs have become mere words, because they have no place in the teaching of natural science about the human corpse.

As long as we limit this teaching to a theory of knowledge, it is more or less harmless. If, however, we consider the human being as a totality and ask what happens to the human being when he or she is influenced by such a life, the question is one of life and death. And this we must not ignore, must not evade. The forces active in the children in our classrooms are quite different from those we learned about. We no longer know anything of what is active in them; we are separated from them by a gulf.

Yes, the Greeks would have considered our talk about the elements nonsensical. What did they say? They believed not that the structure of the world consists of some one hundred elements but that four elements—earth, air, fire, and water—are interacting in it. Our academics, our professors, the leaders of our culture and education will tell us: "This is a childish world conception. We left it behind and no longer bother with it." Someone who has begun to think a little will tell us: "Oh well, we too are working with these things. Today we call them aggregate conditions—solid, gaseous, liquid. We see warmth differently from the naive way the Greeks did. Yes, we have them all, but we have developed them correctly. Of course, we admire the Greeks for their knowledge." This is a benevolent, patronizing, condescending attitude: "We are fortunate in having progressed so far, in having discovered all these elements, whereas the ancients used to practice all sorts of animism and talked of earth, air, fire, and water."

But these leaders are wrong. There is a deeper meaning to the conception of the Greeks. When the Greeks spoke of earth, air, fire, and water, they did not look at them as we do today. If you had asked one of those people who lived within the Greek world conception—and there were still a good number of them in the fifteenth century, the later ones having read about it in books; our modern people sometimes take a look at it without understanding it—if you had asked one of them: "What is your idea of fire, of warmth?" the Greek would have answered: "I think of fire as being warm and dry." "What about air?" "I see air as warm and damp." The Greek did not think of the physical properties in fire and air but rather formed an idea. This idea contained the sub-ideas: warm and dry, warm and damp. The Greeks did not limit themselves to the physical appearance but imagined the elements as inner qualities. One had to raise oneself to something that could not be seen by physical eyes, that had to be grasped by thinking, in order to get to a knowledge of the elements, of what one then called the elements.

What did they achieve by this? They arrived at an understanding that corresponded to the etheric in the human being—the etheric body in its effectiveness. This understanding of the elements as inner qualities allowed them to experience the etheric body. Their experience was not that of being in the etheric body but rather in how the etheric body worked in the physical. It is not possible to achieve this understanding merely by studying the interactions of oxygen and carbon intellectually. It is impossible to arrive at an understanding of the way the etheric body is working in the physical if one only studies the interactions of carbon, hydrogen, oxygen, and sulfur. Such studies take one away from the activities of the etheric, keep one within the physical. This means that one remains in the sphere in which the processes in the human being take place after death. The life processes, in which the etheric body is working in the physical, can only be understood by imagining warm and dry, cold and damp, warm and damp—by inwardly grasping the qualities with which the etheric body takes hold of the physical, by having this living comprehension of nature in the four elements. This is not a childish idea that regards only the physical but one that regards the working of the etheric. And this idea was lost in later times.

But this has an effect on the whole of the human being. Think about it. People are growing up, are told that the world consists of one hundred or so elements—iodine, sulfur, selenium, tellurium, and so forth—all whirling into each other. This affects our feelings, to the extent that we, as human beings, are removed from the process. The elements are there, and we are not part of any of them.

One could have the justified idea of being a part of the other way of looking at the world, of looking at the four elements—earth, air, fire, and water—in the ancient Greek way: earth as cold and dry, air as warm and damp, fire as warm and dry, water as cold and damp. When one imagines these qualities and makes them live in oneself, they grip one—qualitatively. One becomes permeated by them, they take hold of the limbs; they take hold of us. Such ideas that reach as far as into the limbs make us into beings different from beings for whom the ideas affect the limbs only after death. The corpses in the graves may well feel in line with the one hundred or so elements that combine according to chemical laws. But such a concept does not do anything for the life of human beings. By contrast, in having this idea of the four elements, we perceive ourselves in our etheric bodies.

You see from such reflections that education has really become quite unnecessary today for us human beings. We have a culture, an education, that at best prepares us to be able to function outwardly, mechanically, to maintain the status quo in society. For this we are prepared. As human beings we get nothing. Our education does not reach our limbs but remains stuck in the intellect. It does not affect our feelings and will.

If we wish to have any effect at all, we must resort to sermons and the like. We must approach people from without. But we do not give them anything that affects their inner life. The way we deal with the young today involves a terrible untruth. We tell them to be good without providing the means whereby they can be good. All they can do is to obey us as their authority. If we can manage to cow people throughout their lives in one way or another, some order can be maintained. The police will deal with the recalcitrants.

Head knowledge has no meaning for the inner life. This is the reason for our impotence in relating to the young at the important time in their lives when they are supposed to connect the spirit and soul to the physical/corporeal, to bring them into a reciprocal relationship. What indeed are today's adults to do with the young who wish to relate spirit and soul to the physical, to the life around them?

This is the situation we shall take as our starting point in tomorrow's talk, when we shall further acquaint ourselves with this problem. My intention today has been to evoke in you the feeling that as soon as we are supposed to find a way to the hearts of children at a definite and important time in their lives, we are dealing with the important issue of a world conception.

7

STUTTGART / JUNE 18, 1921

Yesterday we began with a subject I referred to as a kind of exploration of conscience that is appropriate for our time and especially necessary for the teacher of children in their fourteenth and fifteenth years. Not only ought this age that outwardly manifests in sexual maturity to be dealt with at the actual time; it ought to be kept in mind throughout the school years. Because our own education—or miseducation—was such that as a result there can be no real understanding of children, especially children in this age group, this kind of higher exploration of conscience has become essential.

We can visualize this situation by proceeding as follows. Let us consider the human being between twenty-one and twenty-eight years. Spiritual science speaks of the birth of the ego, the time when the ego actually comes fully into its own in life. We emphasized the fact that the ego of the girl at about the fourteenth or fifteenth year is absorbed into the astral body, is therefore not yet independent, while the girl's astral body has already attained a certain independence at this age. The ego of the boy, we said, is not absorbed into the astral body; it leads a kind of withdrawn life. And I explained that both these tendencies, these characteristics, can indeed be seen as the result of the inner human development.

But when the I, the ego, fully comes into its own at about the twenty-first year, this shows itself in one human being looking for and finding others, and this in the fullest sense of the word: other human beings. This is such a specific characteristic of this age. When, let's say, a twenty-four-year-old finds a twenty-one-year-old—but not younger than twenty-one or older than twenty-eight—the two will be in an equal, reciprocal relationship in all areas: spirit, soul, body. During this age, we really interact with, relate to others in this age group as equals.

This observation is of special significance for anyone who wishes to be involved in education. All the psychological fiddle-faddle that is frequently practiced is a mere playing with clever words. If we today wish to understand life, we have to observe such things as this special nuance that is present in human beings when they meet one another between their twenty-first and twenty-eighth years.

Let us now consider other age groups: a youth between the age of fourteen and twenty-one and someone between twenty-eight and thirty-five. Regardless of their sexes, it will not be possible for them to relate fully as equals. And yet, provided certain conditions we shall presently discuss are met, a significant relationship can be established between them. If a youth aged fourteen, fifteen, or sixteen meets a twenty-eight-, twenty-nine-, or thirty-year-old person, the matter is as follows. Engendered by the astral body, the physical development between the ages of fourteen and twenty-one, the characteristic outer behavior, the improving skills, the ideals, the way the young find their way into outer life—this is subject to unconsciousness, just as the physical life proceeds unconsciously when developing to the outside.

The same development emerges as a soul form in the inner life of those between the ages of twenty-eight and thirty-five. This is the reason why persons in this age group are especially predestined for understanding, for feeling, the processes taking place in adolescents. And adolescents are especially suited to look up to people between the ages of twenty-eight and thirty-five, because they can see inwardly active in those between the ages of twenty-eight and thirty-five what is in themselves more or less unconsciously manifesting physically in connection to the world outside.

The knowledge of the connection between these age groups was still very much present in ancient Greece. It was instinctively experienced. When Greek children looked up to the older ones they felt instinctively, not fully consciously: "They have in their souls what we have in our bodies; we see something coming to us from them in a refined way, what we have in our physical bodies." And the twenty-eight or twenty-nine-year-old Greeks took immense pleasure in what they saw developing and manifesting in the fourteen-, fifteen-, and sixteen-year-olds. There was this real relation between age groups, this instinctive life—not as in our culture, where people only relate in an abstract way—in which one was important for the other person by virtue of one's age. The Greeks still experienced this instinctive relationship in an extraordinarily strong way, and it really affected their social life.

Try to visualize this situation in Greece. The child grew up, revered a person in his or her early thirties. On reaching the age of twenty-one, the child strongly felt: "Now I have to find someone of my own age." This resulted in a manifoldness and also an inwardness.

It also gave the social life a certain structure. We must emphasize this point especially today, when this instinctive life is no longer present in human beings, when especially the teachers of adolescents do not know what to do with them. We cannot find answers to this problem because—as I said yesterday—we were not given such ideas and concepts that could affect our feelings to the extent that the instincts we lost during the natural course of evolution could in a more conscious way be revived.

Without our preoccupation with anthroposophical spiritual science, by which such feelings, such refined feelings, can again be stimulated, we would gradually produce even deeper gulfs between the older children and ourselves. All we could then do is to command, to order them, to do this or that. Should we fail in this we could have recourse to the police or some other authority who would then threaten the disobedient. We cannot establish an inner relationship between teachers and students unless—however theoretical this may sound—we stimulate such thoughts in our whole being that can again awaken in us, but now consciously, what the instinctive life used to provide for people in the past.

Because of this difference in world conception, as I told you yesterday, what we are learning today about our world—that the different substances and properties in nature are combinations of some one hundred or so elements—is valid for us only after death, for our corpses in their graves. The chemical and physical interactions concern not the living human being but only the corpse, which disintegrates according to the laws we find in the combinations of these elements.

By contrast we can point to the views held especially by the ancient Greeks, and still by people as late as the fourth century—views that are today dismissed as childish, as I said yesterday. But these views, correctly understood, provided the people with something else: the way they regarded the four elements—earth, air, fire, and water. As I pointed out, they did not regard the four elements as pictures of coarse sense impressions, coarse physical matter; they regarded them qualitatively. Fire contained at the same time the qualities warm and dry; they thought of water as cold and damp. These living concepts that they connected to the elements could then be applied in several ways.

They applied them in the way they thought about their connection to earth, air, fire, and water—in which they saw pictures, quite definite pictures. They could apply them to the way, in the human being, that the etheric body activates the mixing and demixing, synthesis and analysis of matter. They could understand how the etheric body is working in the physical between birth and death. All we can do, by contrast, is to limit our thinking to the processes in our corpses after death, processes in keeping with the physical and chemical laws. The Greeks and their followers, as far as into the fifteenth century, could think of the working of the etheric in the physical body, by developing qualitatively the properties of fire as warm and dry, of water as cold and damp, of earth as cold and dry, and so on.

By applying these four elements to the human being, one works in a far more living, inner way, which enables one to imagine the etheric body's participation in the physical substances. By imagining this participation as living processes one becomes inwardly much more mobile, more alive, especially if one adds to one's imagination something else the Greeks still understood in a living way. They imagined the following [a drawing is made].

You see, today we have the surface of the earth, on it the green plants. How do we today imagine the processes taking place in the world of plants? Here, too, our knowledge is limited to the explanations of the chemical analyses and syntheses taking place in the one hundred or so elements. Anything else is denied, or the attempt is made to see it according to the analogy with reciprocal mineral interaction. One would like to see the interaction of chlorophyll, the green color of the plant, with some outer entities during the plant's growth as a process similar to that taking place in a test tube. This is not actually said in so many words, but this mode of thinking has become widespread. The plants are being studied according to their mineral properties.

The Greeks, on the other hand, even though they did not express it concisely, said: "When a plant grows, the cold and dry qualities of the earth are working from below upward. Once the plant has emerged from the earth, when it grows leaves and blossoms with their beautiful colors, we see all this as the effect of water and air, in the way we imagine their qualities; and permeating all of it is the effect of fire. Everywhere in the environment there is this interaction, this intermingling of warm and dry, cold and damp, warm and damp, and all of it, all this qualitative interweaving and interwhirling of dry, cold, damp, and warm across the surface of the earth affects the plant life."

We just have to see this. If we do, and then if we look away from the plants to the human being, to the way the etheric body is active within the human being, we shall there see something that is similar to plant life. When we look at the total life of the plant, we are inwardly stirred and stimulated, let me say, to participate in this life of the plant, in this objective life. The Greeks felt this. Outside, they said, "everything is blossoming, thriving, growing, and ever changing. All this is also working in me." The activity of the Greek's own etheric body, imagined in this way, was not beyond experience. The Greek reflected: "I am no stranger to what constitutes the etheric body in me. Certainly, I cannot see it. But by looking at everything that is growing around me, I experience these activities also within me."

And if such a Greek—not in a present incarnation but as an ancient Greek—were alive today, and if a modern chemist were to tell him: "Your ideas are nonsensical, childish ones. We have left them behind, discovered not four, but some one hundred elements—hydrogen, oxygen, chlorine, bromine, iodine, and so on"—the Greek would have responded by saying: "I have no quarrel with this, there is no harm in it. But it is no more than a specialized, detailed study of my understanding of the cold and dry qualities of the earth. You have not got beyond the knowledge of the cold and dry properties of the earth. You know nothing of water, fire, and air. You haven't got the faintest idea of what goes on in the world of plants, of the etheric life in yourself. You cannot even speak about the plants, because your knowledge of the elements cannot give you any idea of life, of what is working in the life of plants."

Try to feel another ring to our words, how they will be living, as soon as we experience within us the greening, growing processes in the world around us, once these processes cease to be incomprehensible to us. And I can assure you that once it has again become a living experience, incorporated into education, this inner nuance permeating our words will not be limited to affecting the soul abstractly but will put color into faces again. It will transform the whole human being, will have a harmonizing effect. The teacher's words will have a healthy ring to them, will have a different effect, regardless of anything else. All the other theories that tell us what to do, how things ought to be, are basically nothing but plants cultivated in conservatories. Real education must grow naturally. It must be absorbed into our mental images and feelings in the same way that nourishment is absorbed by the processes active in our blood and nerves, thus growing together with us in our organism.

It is essentially the beginning of folly to tell someone what to do. It is as if we were to say to a stove, "You were put into the room, and it is your duty as a stove to warm the room." A stove is filled with firewood, which is then lit, but education needs a true knowledge of the human being that can then come alive in the whole person, that can reach our feelings and also our will. It is necessary for us to develop such a knowledge.

The Greeks, though, did not limit themselves to the observation of the life in plants. They looked up to the cosmos, where initially they perceived the circling planets—from the moon to Saturn, as they said.

The Greeks observed the stars and felt: "Here on earth, where I am surrounded by the plants, I am permeated by the effects of fire, air, and water. The plants are permeated by fire, air, and water. What I see there also works rhythmically in me. I actually bear the whole year in me. As the processes of dry and damp and of cold and warm harmonize in the greening and decaying plants, so my etheric body works in me. The only difference is the fact that I have in me a whole world, so that what happens outside during the course of a year takes place within me in shorter rhythms."

The Greeks felt themselves as living beings within the world, felt themselves belonging to the earth beings. But then they said: "As far as the plants are concerned I can see the beginning of the interaction of earth, air, fire, and water. The etheric then extends upward with its effects. It is now met by the cosmos, by the effects of the stars, initially by the effects of the planets, on fire, air, and water. Without the planets, I would have an etheric body, the plants would exist. But I would not, for example, be able to develop the front part of my brain without the forces of Saturn, working from without. I would not have a larynx without the Mars forces, working from without. I would not have a heart without the forces raying in from without."

These thoughts prompted the further reflection: "Forces are raying in from without. The etheric is raying outward. But the forces that constitute me are raying in from indefinite cosmic distances—forces that are modified through the influence of the planets, forces extending inward from beyond the plant world." The Greeks felt: "I could not have the front part of my brain, could not have a larynx, heart, or stomach without

Saturn, Mars, the sun, or Mercury." Through their organs, the Greeks felt themselves as much a part of the wide cosmos as they felt themselves part of earth, air, fire, and water in the etheric body. And they saw the cosmic forces whirling through each other in earth, air, fire, and water in a way that allowed the heart, the lungs, and the other organs to develop.

The Greeks felt themselves to be physical products not just of the earth but of the whole cosmos. "Here I am." they could say, "standing beside a plant. But cosmic forces are active in me. These forces also affect the plants, but merely from without. They cannot enter the plants, cannot produce organs in them. But they penetrate me and produce in me everything I share with the animals. In regard to my organizing the effects of the cosmos, I can reach as far as the zodiac. There I have exhausted the sphere in which I can observe everything that extends into my animal nature and into the animals around me. I see the animals in their characteristic forms—I see a lion, for example. In the lion I can see a definite interaction between the planets and the fixed stars, which allows me to understand why a lion has this particular shape and these particular features. The same applies to the other animals. Learning to understand the nature of the animals around me, I learn to understand the astral body. I also experience the astral body within myself, just as I experience the etheric—what is in the plants—within myself. Together with the animals of the earth, I am not merely a creature of earth but a member of the cosmos, of that which pulsates through the cosmos as a result of the existence of the stars."

Such a perception of the world can indeed permeate a human being, permeate one's feelings, so that one may say: "Certainly, I can see objects formed according to mineral laws. But these do not include me. Neither am I a part of the plant world. And I am certainly not part of the animal world.

I cannot live on the earth merely through the forces rising from the earth." Feeling oneself within the whole of the universe essentially constituted the element in which the Greeks used to live, albeit yet instinctively.

The ego was then sought outside the circle of the zodiac, in a sphere that was pure spirit, for which a physical correlate could not be found except in its outer picture, the sun. This is the idea of the sun held by the people of still earlier times; it had become somewhat decadent during the Greek cultural period.

Our physicists and astronomers imagine the sun as a huge gaseous ball some twenty million miles away in the universe. This huge cosmic gas stove—without walls—radiates light and warmth in all directions. It is the only explanation, the sole idea for us—if we wish to be experts and not naive dilettantes. Indeed it is only an "expert," a "specialist," who could hold such a view. You will get closer to the truth by imagining the following. Imagine yourself surrounded by light. Light is everywhere. But nowhere is there an object that reflects this light. The light will then not be reflected to you; the light-filled space will be dark. You will not see anything; you will be surrounded by total darkness. Were there nothing but light, we would experience total darkness. Light only returns to us if it is caught by something; otherwise we cannot see it. In a light-filled room is total darkness.

A better age than ours certainly entertained this idea. Its people knew that the sun was not a gigantic gas stove, that there was not merely an empty space up there, but less than space, a negative space. Our physicists would get the surprise of their lives if they were to travel to the sun. They would not find the imagined gas ball, would perceive nothing, not even space, but merely left-out space, an energy or force that absorbs space. This force exists. Space is everywhere. We just have to be able to imagine the "less-than-space." In the meantime, we at least know that "less-than-no-money" means debts.

Space has its boundaries, and negative space collects the light, which cannot pass through the negative emptiness, but is rayed back. Thus the sun becomes visible. Light is everywhere. What we see as the sun is only an entity that rays back, an apparatus that reflects the light. The origin of this light is, according to the Greeks, beyond the region of the zodiac. The light enters from cosmic distances and not from perceptible space. But it is collected, made visible, through the sun.

This, so the Greeks said, is connected with the development of the ego, whose origin is in regions higher than the planets. The sun is connected with the ego by virtue of the fact that the sun is less than space, emptier than space—at the place of the sun all matter ceases to be and spirituality can enter. It was because the Greeks understood the spiritual nature of the sun that they felt themselves so very much related to it.

Something of this living feeling, of this entering into the spirit by looking up to the cosmos, was still consciously experienced as late as the sixth century, especially during the middle of the fourth century. And because of the living feeling, events were described as resulting from the influence not of the planets but of the hierarchical beings who move what can be outwardly perceived as the planets. This living idea is necessary if we wish to arrive at a different experience of ourselves, imparted into the world as human beings.

If now we take a look at the animal kingdom from this point of view, we may say that this is also within us. It produces our organs. But the animals I see are enclosed in definite forms. I have not become such a form. I do not look like a lion, a bull, an ox, or a pig. I have in me all the animals as synthesis; I have within me the disposition for all of them. If the effect of the sun had not equalized it all, I should be somebody in whom the whole of the animal kingdom were thrown together, whirling, all the animals rooting into each other. It is the effect of the sun that equalizes it, that brings it to a state of balance.

And what is the result of this fact—that I bear within me the dispositions for all the animals, but in a suppressed way? It allows me to think forms, imaginations. The animals are outwardly shaped according to their imaginations; they are living imaginations, move about as imaginations. Looking at the animals I can see the world of imagination. The same forms are in me. They have become thought pictures in me, because I have not assumed their outer shape, have not made them spatial.

If we were to go even further back in time, before Thales, we would find an exact knowledge taught in mystery centers. Plato recorded this knowledge in his esoteric writings. We may describe it as follows. What is logic? Living logic is zoology! What comes to expression in the animal kingdom harmonizes itself in us and, according to our predisposition, assumes a spiritually abstract form, thus producing in us living thought activity. It is the animal kingdom that is active in our life of thoughts. Ergo, logic is zoology.

This knowledge was later replaced by the Socratism of Aristotle, and the consciousness was lost. The beginning of abstract logic came when the living relation of *elective affinities* gave way to the relation of judgment, the abstract connection of concepts—as we see them expressed in Aristotle's logic, a logic that can drive the student preoccupied with it to despair, because in it can be found nothing concrete on which to build, nothing to hang on to.

We feel, we think, we develop concepts because we have within us what is spread out, outside of us, in the animal kingdom. If we develop this view, we impart ourselves into the world in a way that is quite different. Will and feelings are then vitalized in a way that is quite different. We feel ourselves related to the nature kingdoms. And we gradually experience not only the etheric but also the astral activity in ourselves.

If we are not limited by the abstract concepts taught everywhere today, but if we are inwardly stimulated by positive forms, and if we are then confronted by the fourteen- and fifteen-year-old children, we learn to observe them. What we inwardly receive will then direct our eyes and ears to the way we ought to conduct the next lesson. Our eyes are led and guided, our ears are led and guided, and only in this way will our observation of what is going on in the fourteen- and fifteen-year old students be stimulated. If we do not have this stimulation, if we do not permeate ourselves with such a spiritual science that enters our life of feelings, we confront these youngsters—as people used to say when I was young—"as the ox confronts Sunday, after having eaten grass all week."

It is this that we must give our culture, our civilization, our sciences, so that they can become real, and not only a sum total of names, a mere nominalism, so that they can kindle in us something that has meaning and reality. This will allow us to observe human beings. I do not mean that we ought to proceed craftily, recording their behavior in notebooks. No, the positive forms will come to us as though by themselves when we observe in this way. We shall arrive at a judgment of each child, need not speak about it, because it will be mobile within us. We can then raise it to consciousness, and we shall conduct our lessons according to the numerous judgments that live and surge in us, as the whole of the animal kingdom is living in true thought forms.

Just think what it would mean if we had to know everything, if we had to have a clear notion of how the lion is eating a lamb, if we had to be fully conscious of that. By the same token, we cannot judge everything in our environment, cannot raise everything to an explicit consciousness. But it can be there; we can act accordingly. If we have not taken our starting point from the knowledge that only reckons with abstract concepts and abstract natural laws and that cannot possibly raise itself to such positive thought forms, then we can stand among our students and act appropriately. But how can we have anything other than such a starting point if we imagine the big gas stove without walls boiling away in the universe. Such a concept cannot lead to a better understanding of human beings.

All of this must lead to the deep exploration of conscience, to our telling ourselves that unless we make every effort to permeate our life of instincts and feelings with spiritual science, we can no longer understand children in their fourteenth and fifteenth years. We learn to understand them only by progressing to such a knowledge. This is what is meant by our ever emphasizing that anthroposophy is pedagogy. In other words, anthroposophy becomes pedagogy when one gets to the stage at which one can educate. All that is needed is to take from the depths of the soul what has been put into it through anthroposophy, if it is to be applied to education. What I mean to say is that if the qualities present in each human being are given a pedagogical direction, the anthroposophical understanding of the human being will also become a true pedagogy.

Yesterday I said to the teachers of the tenth grade that they should begin with a certain knowledge of the human being. Such a knowledge wishes to make us understand that we ought to place the human being again into the whole universe, according to body, soul, and spirit. We really should—if we are true teachers working on the basis of this knowledge of the human being—study anatomy and physiology, learn everything that has been produced in these fields by centuries of spiritless work. But these books should be no more than sources of information, and we should never omit to pour into them the knowledge we can gain from anthroposophy.

Only this approach will shed light on the information that emerges from such books, on what is generally held to be true today. You must have a different attitude toward this literature than other people. Certainly you will be called arrogant and worse, but you will have to accept this treatment today. You will have to live with it. You will have to see in the offerings of modern science merely the source for information—just as a member of the ancient Greek culture, if such a one were to come to life today and read a book on chemistry, would say: "The things I know about the earth, that it is dry and cold, that it affects plant growth, this you specialize for me. To learn about the details is interesting. But you have no knowledge of the totality of life; you merely know a quarter of it."

We must return to a knowledge that enters our feelings and will, that permeates our whole being, that is for soul and spirit similar to the blood for the physical. Then becoming different human beings, we shall also become true teachers. The teaching profession cannot tolerate the automatization of the human being, which is the result of the various artificially grown greenhouse plants in educational theories. There are even experiments today that are supposed to lead to new concepts—experiments that show how memory works, how the will and even the thoughts are developing and running their course, harmless games that might even produce results. We need not be against games, those of children or those of the laboratory. What matters, however, is that we oppose the narrowing of the horizon that such experiments produce.

8

STUTTGART / JUNE 19, 1921

During our reflections on education, we have had to emphasize that our work as teachers depends on the manner in which we ourselves develop and find our way to the world. And we have had to single out the frequently characterized age of thirteen, fourteen, fifteen years—for which our own correct preparation for our lessons is especially important.

But we also have to organize all our educational activities in such a way that we prepare the children for this age. Everything depends on their developing a definite relation to the world. This relation to the world announces itself especially at the age we are now discussing, when both girls and boys begin to incline toward ideals, toward something in life that is to be added to the physical, sense-perceptible world. Even in their obnoxious teenage behavior we can see this inclination toward a supersensible, ideal life—toward, as it were, a higher idea of purpose: Life must have a meaning! This is a deeply seated conviction for the human being. And we have to reckon with this "Life must have a meaning, a purpose!"

It is especially important at this age that we do not channel this basic inner maxim—life must have a purpose—into the wrong direction. Boys at this age are often seen as being filled with all sorts of ideas and hope for life, so that they easily get the notion that this or that has to be so or so. Girls get into the habit of making certain judgments about life. They are, especially at this age, sharply critical of life, convinced that they know what is right and wrong, fair and unfair. They make definite judgments and are convinced that life has to offer something that, coming from ideas deep down in human nature, must then be realized in the world. This inclination toward ideals and ideas is indeed strongly present at this age.

It is up to us whether, during the whole of the elementary school years beginning in first grade, we manage to allow the children to grow into this life of ideals, this imaginative life. A necessary condition is that we ourselves be able to permeate our whole being with such principles that allow us a correct understanding of the way children develop. Through anthroposophy we get a theoretical knowledge of the three most important aspects. Up to the seventh year, when the change of teeth occurs, children are essentially imitators. They develop, we may say, by doing what they see done in their environment. All their activities are basically imitations. Then during the time of the change of teeth, children begin to feel the need for an authority, the need to be told what to do. Thus, while before the change of teeth children accept the things that are done in the environment as a matter of course, copying the good *and* the bad, the true *and* the false, now they no longer feel the need to imitate but know that they can carry out what they are told to do and not to do. Then again, at puberty the children begin to feel that they can now make judgments themselves, but they still want to be supported by authorities of their own choosing: "This person may be listened to; I can accept his or her opinions and judgments."

It is important that we allow the children to grow into this natural relation to authority in the right way. To do this we must understand the meaning and significance of the imitative instinct. What does it actually tell us? The imitative instinct cannot be understood if we do not see children as coming from the spiritual world. An age that limits itself to seeing children as the result of hereditary traits cannot really understand the nature of imitation. It cannot arrive at the simplest living concepts, concepts capable of life.

The science of this age sees the chemical, the physical world, how the elements, enumerated in chemistry, analyze and synthesize; it discovers, in progressing to the sphere of life—but working with it in a synthetic and analytic way—processes that correspond identically with those in the human corpse. Such a science, applying the same process that can be observed during the natural decomposing of the corpse, finds the same elements in the living organism: carbon, oxygen, nitrogen, and the rest. And it discovers these elements living in the form we know as albumen. The scientists now try to discover how the carbon, nitrogen, hydrogen, and oxygen in the albumen can be synthesized in a living way. And they hope to discover one day how these elements—C, N, H, and O—develop a definite structure by virtue of being together in albumen.

But this procedure will never lead to an understanding of albumen as the basis of life. In characterizing albumen in the cell in this way we follow a wrong direction. The reality is quite different. The natural, instinctive forces that hold the substances together, that bring about specific forms in, for example, a mountain crystal, a cube of pyrite, or other minerals, change to a chaotic condition during the creation of albumen. We should, in our study of albumen, instead of paying attention to more complicated laws, observe how these forces in their reciprocal relation paralyze themselves, cease to be active in the albumen, are no longer in it. Instead of structure, we should look for chaos, dissolution. We should tell ourselves: The substances in their reciprocal activities change to a chaotic condition when they pass to the stage in which they appear as albumen; then they enter an undefined, vague stage, cease to influence one another, enter a stage in which they become open to another influence.

In the general life processes, this chaotic condition is still kept somewhat in check through the mineral processes in the organism. The cells in our brain, lungs, and liver, as far as they are albumen, are still affected by the forces we receive from our food. There the chaotic condition is not present. But in the cells that later become our reproductive cells, the cell substance is protected from the influence of food, protected from the forces we receive from food. In our reproductive cells there is almost complete chaos; all mineral substances are completely destroyed, ruined. Reproductive cells are produced in human beings, in animals, and in plants by virtue of the fact that the terrestrial effects, the mineral activities, are through a laborious process destroyed, ruined. This process allows the organism to become receptive to the work of the cosmos. Cosmic forces can now work into the organism from every direction. These cosmic forces are initially influenced by the reproductive cells of the other sex, adding the astral to the etheric. We may say that as the mineral elements demineralize themselves, the possibility arises for the cosmic laws to enter on this detour through the chaotic condition of the albumen, whereas ordinarily in the mineral world we find the terrestrial influencing the terrestrial.

Natural science will never comprehend the nature of albumen as long as it endeavors to find in the organic molecule a structure that is simply more complicated than that which occurs in the inorganic molecule. Today's chemistry and physiology are mainly concerned with discovering the structure of atoms in different bodies, atoms which assume ever more complex forms, culminating in that of the albumen. The molecule of albumen does not tend toward greater complexity, however, but toward the dissolution of mineral structure, so that extraterrestrial—and not terrestrial—forces can influence it.

Our thinking is here confused by modern science. We are led to a thinking that is—in its most important aspects—in no way connected to reality. Our modern knowledge of the properties of albumen prevents us from raising our thoughts to the reality that something enters the human being that does not come from heredity but via the detour from the cosmos. Today's idea of albumen leaves no room for the concept of the pre-existence of the human being.

We have to understand the tremendous importance of learning, as teachers, to distance ourselves from the basic tenets of modern science. With the basic tenets of modern science one can bamboozle people, but one cannot teach with them. Our universities do not teach at all. What do they do? There is a faculty that enforces its position through the power of unions or associations. The students have to congregate there, in order to prepare themselves for life. Nobody would do this. Neither the old nor the young would do this, if it were left to them to develop their innate forces and potential. In order to make them study, compulsion is necessary. They are forced into this situation, incarcerated for a while, if they wish to prepare themselves for a profession. And because of this, these institutions do not think of relaxing their power. It is a childish notion to believe such institutions, the last outposts at which compulsory membership clings—the compulsory membership of all the other unions no longer existing—it is hard to believe such institutions are in the forefront of progress. They are the last place of recourse for finding answers. Everywhere else the enforced measures and rules of the Middle Ages have been done away with. In the way today's universities are conducted, they are in no way different from the guilds of the Middle Ages. Our universities are the last remnants of the guilds. And since those concerned with these things have no longer any knowledge, any feeling about this development, they enlist the help of show business, especially during such highlights as graduation ceremonies—caps, gowns, and so forth. It is important to see behind these things.

One who today wishes to educate and teach must find other ways in which to become a true human being; one must acquire new ideas of the basic principles. Then one will arrive at the correct understanding of the nature of imitation during early childhood.

During the time in the spiritual world, before conception, the child's soul accepts everything from its spiritual surroundings as a matter of course. After birth the child continues this activity that the soul became used to in the spiritual world. In the child's imitating we can see that this habit from before birth has not been lost; it has only taken a different turn. Before conception the child was concerned with development from within; now the world outside is confronted. We may use the following picture to help us understand this difference. Before conception the child was as though within a ball; now the child looks at this ball from outside. The world one sees with one's physical eyes is the outside of what one saw previously from within. Imitation is an instinctive urge for the child in all activities, a continuation of the child's experience in the spiritual world; it is through imitation that the child develops an initial relation to the spiritual world in the physical world.

Just think what this means! Keep in mind that the very young child wants to face the outer world according to the principles that are valid in the spiritual world. During these early years, the child develops a sense for the true and, connecting to the world in this way, arrives at the conviction: "Everything around me is as true as the things I so clearly perceived in the spiritual world." The child develops the sense for the true before beginning school. We still observe the last phases of this conviction when the child enters school, and we must receive the child's sense for the true in the right way. Otherwise we blunt it instead of developing it further.

Consider now the situation of children entering first grade and forced to adapt to the conventional way people read and write today—an activity that is external to human nature. Our modern way of reading and writing is abstract, external to human nature. Not so long ago, the forms of the letters were quite different. They were pictures—that is, they did not remind one of the reality, but they depicted the reality. But by teaching the Roman alphabet, we take the children into a quite foreign element, which they can no longer imitate.

If we show the children pictures, teach them how to draw artistic, picturelike forms, encourage them to make themselves into pictures of the world through a musical element that is adapted to child nature, we then continue what they had been doing by themselves before starting school. If, on the other hand, we teach by instructing them to copy an abstract "I" or "O," the children will have no cause to be interested, no cause for inwardly connecting with our teaching. The children must in a certain way be connected with what they are doing. And the sense of imitation must now be replaced by the sense of beauty. We must begin to work from all directions toward the healthy separation from imitation, to allow the children's imitation to give way to a correct, more outer relation to the world. The children must grow into beings who copy the outer world beautifully. And we must now begin to consider two as yet rather undifferentiated aspects—namely, the teaching of physical skills and the teaching of such things that are more concerned with knowledge, with the development of concepts.

What are children actually doing when they sing or make eurythmic movements? They disengage themselves from imitating, yet the imitating activity continues in a certain way. The children move. Singing and listening to music are essentially inner movements—the same process as in imitation. And when we let children do eurythmy, what are we actually doing then? Instead of giving them sticks of crayon with which to write an "A" or an "E"—an activity with which they have a purely cognitive connection—we let the children write into the world, through their own human form, what constitutes the content of language. The human being is not directed to abstract symbols but allowed to write into the world what can be inscribed through his or her organism. We thus allow the human being to continue the activity of prenatal life. And if we then do not take recourse to abstract symbols when we teach reading and writing, but do this through pictures, we do not distance ourselves from the real being when we must activate it, we do not let the human being get fully away from it. Through effort and practice we employ the whole of the human being.

I want you to be aware of what we are doing with the children in regard to their activities. On the one hand, we have the purely physiological physical education lessons. There the children are trained and tamed—we merely use different methods—as animals are. But spirit and soul are excluded from our considerations. On the other hand, we have lessons that are unconnected with the human body. We have progressed to the point at which, in writing and reading, the more delicate movements of the fingers, arms, and eyes are made so active that the rest of the organism is not participating in them. We literally cut the human being in half.

But when we teach eurythmy, when the movements contain the things the children are to learn in writing, we bring these two parts—body and soul/spirit—closer together. And in the children's artistic activities, when the letters emerge from pictures, we have one and the same activity—now, however, tinged by soul and spirit—as in eurythmic movements or in listening to singing, a process in which the children's own consciousness is employed. We join body, soul, and spirit, allowing the child to be a totality.

By proceeding in this way, we shall, of course, find ourselves reproached by parents in parent/teacher meetings. We only have to learn to deal with them appropriately when they ask us, for example, to transfer their sons to a class with a male teacher. They would, so they say, have a greater respect for a male teacher. "My son is already eight years old and cannot spell correctly." They blame the female teacher for that, believing that a male teacher would be more likely to drill the child in this subject.

Such erroneous opinions, which keep being voiced in our school community, must be checked; we have to correct them and enlighten the parents. But we must not shock them. We cannot speak to them in the way we speak among ourselves. We cannot say to them: "You ought to be grateful for the fact that your son cannot read and write fluently at the age of nine. He will as a result read and write far better later on. If he could read and write to perfection already at age nine, he would later turn into an automaton, because he would have been inoculated with a foreign element. He would turn into an automaton, a robot."

Children whose writing and reading activities are balanced by something else will grow into full human beings. We have to be gentle with today's grown-ups, who have been influenced by modern culture. We must not shock them; that would not help our cause at all. But we must, tactfully and gently, find a way to convince them that if their child cannot yet read and write fluently at the age of nine, this does not constitute a sin against the child's holy spirit.

If in this way, we guide the child correctly into life—if we don't "cut the child in half" but leave the child's whole being intact, we shall observe an extraordinarily important point in the child's life at the age of nine. The child will relate quite differently to the world outside. It is as though the child were waking up, were beginning to have a new connection to the ego. We should pay attention to this change, at the very beginning. In our time, it is possible for this change to happen earlier. We should observe the new relation to the environment—the child showing surprise, astonishment. Normally this change occurs between the ninth and the tenth years.

If, thoughtfully and inwardly, we ask ourselves what it is that has led to this condition, we shall receive an answer that cannot be accurately expressed in words but can be conveyed by the following analogy. Previously, had we given the child a mirror and had the child seen his or her reflection in it, the child would not have seen it very differently from any other object, would not have been especially affected by it. Imagine a monkey to whom you give a mirror. Have you observed this? The monkey takes hold of the mirror and runs to a place where it can look at it undisturbed, quite calmly. The monkey becomes fascinated by its reflection. Should you try to take the mirror away, that would not be to your advantage. The monkey is absolutely bent on coming to grips with what it sees in the mirror. But you will not notice the slightest change in the monkey afterward. It will not have become vain as a result; the experience does not influence the monkey in this way. The immediate sense impression of the reflected picture fascinates the monkey, but the experience does not metamorphose into anything. As soon as the mirror is taken away, the monkey forgets the whole thing; the experience certainly does not produce vanity.

But a child at the characterized age looking at his or her reflection would be tempted to transform his or her previous way of feeling, to become vain and coquettish. This is the difference between the monkey, satisfied with just seeing itself in the mirror, and the child. Regarding the monkey, the experience does not permanently affect its feeling and will. But for the nine-and-one-half-year-old child, the experience of seeing himself or herself in the mirror produces lasting impressions, influences his or her character in a certain way.

An actual experiment would confirm this result. And a time that wishes to make education into an experimental science—because it cannot think of any other way of dealing with it, because it has lost all inner connection to it—could well feel inclined to make experiments in order to discover the nature of the transition from the ninth to the tenth year. Children would be given mirrors, their reactions would be recorded, learned books would be written, and so forth. But such a procedure is no different for the soul and spirit than the assumption that our ordinary methods cannot solve the mystery of the human being. In order to get answers, we must decide on killing somebody every year, in order to discover the secrets of life at the moment of death. Such scientific experiments are not yet permitted in the physical, sense-perceptible world. But in the realm of soul and spirit, we have progressed to the point that experiments are allowed which paralyze the unhappy victims, paralyze them for life—experiments that ought to be avoided.

Take any of the available books on education and you will find thoughts the very opposite of ours. You will, for example, read things about memory and the nature of sensation, the application of which you ought to avoid in your lessons. Experimental pedagogy occupies itself precisely with such experiments that should be abolished. Everything that should be avoided is experimented with. This is the destructive practice of our current civilization—the wish to discover the processes in the corpse rather than those in life. It is the death processes that experimental pedagogy wishes to study, instead of making the effort to observe life: the way children, in a delicate, subtle way arrive at being astonished at what they see around them, because they are beginning to see themselves placed into the world. It is only at this stage that one arrives at self consciousness, the awareness of one's ego. When one sees it reflected, rayed back from everywhere in the environment, from plants and animals, when one begins to experience them in one's feeling, one relates consciously to them, develops a knowledge through one's own efforts.

This awareness begins to awaken in children at the age of nine and ten. It does not awaken if we avoid the formative activities, if we avoid the meaningful movements in, for example, eurythmy. This is not done today. Children are not educated to do meaningful, sensible things. Like little lambs in a pasture, they are taken to the gymnasium, ordered to move their arms in a certain way, told how to use the various apparati. There is nothing of a spiritual element in such activities—or have you noticed any? Certainly, many beautiful things are said about such activities, but they are not permeated by spirit.

What is the result? At an age that affords the best opportunities for infusing the sense of beauty in children, they do not receive it. The children wish so very much to stand in awe, to be astonished, but the forces for this response are squashed. Take a book on current curricula and their tendencies. The six- and seven-year-old children, on entering school, are treated in a way that makes them impervious to the experiences they ought to have in their tenth year. They don't experience anything. Consequently, the experiences they ought to have pass into the body, instead of into the consciousness. They rumble deep down in the unconscious regions and transform into feelings and instincts of which individuals have no knowledge. People move about in life without being able to connect with it, without discovering anything in it. This is the characteristic of our time. People do not observe anything meaningful in life, because they did not learn as children to see the beautiful in it. All they are to discover are things that in the driest possible sense somehow increase their knowledge. But they cannot find the hidden, mysterious beauty that is present everywhere, and the real connection to life dies away.

This is the course culture is taking. The connection of human beings to nature dies away. If one is permeated by this, if one observes this, then one knows how everything depends on finding the right words, words that will allow children at the age of nine to be astonished. The children expect this from us. If we do not deliver, we really destroy a great deal.

We must learn to observe children, must grow into them with our feelings, be inside them and not rest content with outer experimentation. The situation is really such that we have to say that the development of the human being includes a definite course of life that begins at the moment when in a lower region, as it were, from language, there emerge the words: "I am an 'I.'" One learns to say "I" to oneself at a relatively early age in childhood, but the experience is dreamlike and continues in this dreamy way. The child then enters school. And it is now our task to change this experience. The child wishes, after all, to take a different direction. We must direct the child to artistic activities. When we have done this for a while, the child retraces his or her life and arrives again at the moment of learning to say "I" to himself or herself. The child then continues the process and later, through the event of puberty, again passes through this moment.

We prepare the children for this process by getting them at the age of nine and ten to the point that they can look at the world in wonder, astonishment, and admiration. If we make their sense of beauty more conscious, we prepare the children for the time at and after puberty in such a way that they learn to love correctly, that they develop love in the right way. Love is not limited to sex; sex is merely a special aspect of love. Love is something that extends to everything, is the innermost impetus for action. We ought to do what we love to do. Duty is to merge with love; we should like what we are dutybound to do. And this love develops in the right way only if we go along with the child's inner development. We must, therefore, pay attention to the correct cultivation of the sense of beauty throughout the elementary school years. The sense of truth the children have brought with them; the sense of beauty we have to develop in the way I have described.

That the children have brought the sense of truth with them can be seen in the fact that they have learned to speak before entering school. Language, as it were, incorporates truth and knowledge. We need language if we wish to learn about the world. This fact has led people like Mauthner to assume that everything is already contained in language. People like Mauthner—who wrote the book *Critique of Language*—actually believe that we harm human beings by taking them beyond the point at which they learn to speak. Mauthner wrote his *Critique of Language* because he did not believe in the world, because of his conviction that human beings should be left at a childlike stage, at the time when they learn to speak. Were this idea to become generally accepted, we would be left with a spiritual life that corresponds to that of children at the time when they have learned to speak. This manner of thinking tends toward producing such human beings who remain at the stage of children who have just learned to speak. Everything else is nowadays rejected as ignorance.

What now matters is that we can enter the concept of imitation with our feeling and then to understand the concept of authority as the basis, between us and the children, for the development of the sense for the beautiful. If we manage to do this up to the time of puberty, then as the children are growing into their inclinations toward ideals, the sense for the good is correctly developed. Before puberty it is through us that the children are motivated to do the good; through the reciprocal relationship we must affect the children in this way. It is necessary for the eleven-, twelve-, and thirteen-year-old girls and boys to have the teacher's authority behind them, to feel their teacher's pleasure and satisfaction when they are doing something that is good. And they should avoid bad actions because they feel their teacher would be disappointed. They should be aware of the teacher's presence and in this way unite with him or her. Only at puberty should they emancipate themselves from the teacher.

If we consider the children to be already mature in first grade, if we encourage them to voice their opinions and judgments as soon as they have learned to speak—that is, if we base everything on direct perception [*Anschauung*]—we leave them at the stage of development at which they have just learned to speak, and we deny them any further development. If, in other words, we do not address ourselves to the very real changes at puberty—that the children then leave behind what they were used to doing through our authority—they will not be able later in life to do without it. Children must first experience authority. Then at puberty they must be able to grow beyond it and begin to make and depend on their own judgments.

At this time we really must establish such a connection to the students that each one of them may choose a "hero whose path to Mt. Olympus can be emulated." This change is, of course, connected with some unhappiness and even pain. It is no longer up to the teacher to represent the ideal for the children. The teacher must recognize the change and act accordingly. Before puberty the teacher was able to tell the children what to do. Now the students become rather sensitive to their teachers in their judgments, perceive their weaknesses and shortcomings. We must consciously expose ourselves to this change, must be aware of the students' criticism of their teachers' unwarranted behavior. They become especially sensitive at this age to their teachers' attitudes. If, however, our interest in the students is honest and not egotistical, we shall educate and teach with exactly these possibilities of their feelings in mind. And this will result in a free relationship between us and them.

The effect will be the students' healthy growth into the *true* that was given to them by the spiritual world as a kind of inheritance, so that they can merge with, grow together with, the *beautiful* in the right way, so that they can learn the *good* in the world of the senses, the good they are to develop and bring to expression during their lives. It is really a sin to talk about the true, the beautiful, and the good in abstractions, without showing concretely their relation to the various ages.

Such a short reflection, my dear friends, can of course give us no more than a small segment of what the future holds for us. We can only gradually grow into the tasks we are given. But it really is true that we shall in a certain way grow into them as a matter of course, provided we let ourselves be guided in our work by the forces we can acquire if we see the physical, sense-perceptible world from the standpoint of soul and spirit and if, in observing the world, we do not forget the human being. These things we must do, especially as teachers to whom the young are entrusted.

We really must feel ourselves as a part of the whole universe, wherein the evolution of humankind is playing a major role. For this reason, I would always—at the beginning of the school year—like to see our feelings permeated, as it were, with a healthy sensing of our great task, so that we may in all humility feel ourselves as missionaries in human evolution. In this sense, I always wish such talks to contain also something of a prayer-like element by which we may raise ourselves to the spirit, so that we evoke it not merely intellectually but as a living reality. May we be conscious of the spirit spreading among us like a living cloud that is permeated by soul and spirit; may we feel that the living spirits themselves are called upon through the words we speak among ourselves at the beginning of a new school year, that these living spirits themselves are called forth when we beseech them: "Help us. Bring living spirituality among us. Insert it into our souls, our hearts, so that we may work in the right way."

If you have the sensitivity to appreciate that our words at the beginning of the school year should also be a feeling experience, you will be open to the intention that is connected with our talks. So let me add for you this short meditative formula, to be spoken as follows:

> We resolve to do our work by letting flow into it what from the spiritual world wishes to become human being in us, by way of the soul and spirit as well as of the corporeal-physical organization.

> [*Wir wollen arbeiten, indem wir einfliessen lassen in unsere Arbeit dasjenige, was aus der geistigen Welt heraus auf seelisch-geistige Weise und auch auf leiblich-physische Weise in uns Mensch werden will.*]

Bibliography

Childs, Gilbert. *Understanding Your Temperament! A Guide to the Four Temperaments*. Sophia Books, London, 1995.

Elium, Jeanne & Don Elium. *Raising a Daughter: Parents and the Awakening of a Healthy Woman*. Celestial Arts, Berkeley, CA, 1994.

—— *Raising a Son: Parents and the Making of a Healthy Man*. Beyond Words, Hillsboro, OR, 1992.

Gabert, Erich. *Educating the Adolescent: Discipline or Freedom*. Anthroposophic Press, Hudson, NY, 1988.

Gardner, John Fentress. *Education in Search of the Spirit: Essays on American Education*. Anthroposophic Press, Hudson, NY, 1996.

Gatto, John Taylor. *Dumbing Us Down: The Hidden Curriculum of Compulsory Schooling*. New Society, Philadelphia, 1992.

Koepke, Hermann. *On the Threshold of Adolescence: The Struggle for Independence in the Twelfth Year*. Anthroposophic Press, Hudson, NY, 1992.

Large, Martin. *Who's Bringing Them Up? How to Break the T.V. Habit!* Hawthorn Press, Stroud, UK, 1990.

Sleigh, Julian. *Thirteen to Nineteen: Discovering the Light: Conversations with Parents*. Floris Books, Edinburgh, 1990.

Staley, Betty. *Between Form and Freedom: A Practical Guide to the Teenage Years*. Hawthorn Press, Stroud, UK, 1988.

THE FOUNDATIONS OF WALDORF EDUCATION

THE FIRST FREE WALDORF SCHOOL opened its doors in Stuttgart, Germany, in September, 1919, under the auspices of Emil Molt, the Director of the Waldorf Astoria Cigarette Company and a student of Rudolf Steiner's spiritual science and particularly of Steiner's call for social renewal.

It was only the previous year—amid the social chaos following the end of World War I—that Emil Molt, responding to Steiner's prognosis that truly human change would not be possible unless a sufficient number of people received an education that developed the whole human being, decided to create a school for his workers' children. Conversations with the Minister of Education and with Rudolf Steiner, in early 1919, then led rapidly to the forming of the first school.

Since that time, more than six hundred schools have opened around the globe—from Italy, France, Portugal, Spain, Holland, Belgium, Great Britain, Norway, Finland, and Sweden to Russia, Georgia, Poland, Hungary, Romania, Israel, South Africa, Australia, Brazil, Chile, Peru, Argentina, Japan, and others—making the Waldorf School Movement the largest independent school movement in the world. The United States, Canada, and Mexico alone now have more than 120 schools.

Although each Waldorf school is independent, and although there is a healthy oral tradition going back to the first Waldorf teachers and to Steiner himself, as well as a growing body of secondary literature, the true foundations of the Waldorf method and spirit remain the many lectures that Rudolf Steiner gave on the subject. For five years (1919–24), Rudolf Steiner, while simultaneously working on many other fronts, tirelessly dedicated himself to the dissemination of the idea of Waldorf education. He gave manifold lectures to teachers, parents, the general public, and even the children themselves. New schools were founded. The Movement grew.

While many of Steiner's foundational lectures have been translated and published in the past, some have never appeared in English, and many have been virtually unobtainable for years. To remedy this situation and to establish a coherent basis for Waldorf education, Anthroposophic Press has decided to publish the complete series of Steiner lectures and writings on education in a uniform series. This series will thus constitute an authoritative foundation for work in educational renewal, for Waldorf teachers, parents, and educators generally.

RUDOLF STEINER'S LECTURES (AND WRITINGS) ON EDUCATION

I. *Allgemeine Menschenkunde als Grundlage der Pädagogik. Pädagogischer Grundkurs,* 14 Lectures, Stuttgart, 1919 (GA 293). Previously *Study of Man.* ***Foundations of Human Experience*** (Anthroposophic Press, 1996).

II. *Erziehungskunst Methodische-Didaktisches,* 14 Lectures, Stuttgart, 1919 (GA 294). ***Practical Advice to Teachers*** (Rudolf Steiner Press, 1988).

III. *Erziehungskunst,* 15 Discussions, Stuttgart, 1919 (GA 295). ***Discussions with Teachers*** (Rudolf Steiner Press, 1992).

IV. *Die Erziehungsfrage als soziale Frage,* 6 Lectures, Dornach, 1919 (GA 296). ***Education as a Social Problem*** (Anthroposophic Press, 1969).

V. *Die Waldorf Schule und ihr Geist,* 6 Lectures, Stuttgart and Basel, 1919 (GA 297). ***The Spirit of the Waldorf School*** (Anthroposophic Press, 1995).

VI. *Rudolf Steiner in der Waldorfschule, Vorträge und Ansprachen,* Stuttgart, 1919–1924 (GA 298). ***Rudolf Steiner in the Waldorf School—Lectures and Conversations*** (Anthroposophic Press, 1996).

VII. *Geisteswissenschaftliche Sprachbetrachtungen,* 6 Lectures, Stuttgart, 1919 (GA 299). ***The Genius of Language*** (Anthroposophic Press, 1995).

VIII. *Konferenzen mit den Lehren der Freien Waldorfschule 1919–1924,* 3 Volumes (GA 300). ***Conferences with Teachers*** (Steiner Schools Fellowship, 1986, 1987, 1988, 1989).

IX. *Die Erneuerung der Pädagogisch-didaktischen Kunst durch Geisteswissenschaft,* 14 Lectures, Basel, 1920 (GA 301). ***The Renewal of Education*** (Kolisko Archive Publications for Steiner Schools Fellowship Publications, Michael Hall, Forest Row, East Sussex, UK, 1981).

X. *Menschenerkenntnis und Unterrichtsgestaltung,* 8 Lectures, Stuttgart, 1921 (GA 302). Previously *The Supplementary Course—Upper School* and *Waldorf Education for Adolescence.* ***Education for Adolescents*** (Anthroposophic Press, 1996).

XI. *Erziehung und Unterrricht aus Menschenerkenntnis,* 9 Lectures, Stuttgart, 1920, 1922, 1923 (GA 302a). The first four lectures available as ***Balance in Teaching*** (Mercury Press, 1982); last three lectures as ***Deeper Insights into Education*** (Anthroposophic Press, 1988).

XII. *Die Gesunder Entwicklung des Menschenwesens,* 16 Lectures, Dornach, 1921–22 (GA 303). ***Soul Economy and Waldorf Education*** (Anthroposophic Press, 1986).

XIII. *Erziehungs- und Unterrichtsmethoden auf Anthroposophischer Grundlage,* 9 Public Lectures, various cities, 1921–22 (GA 304). ***Waldorf Education and Anthroposophy I*** (Anthroposophic Press, 1995).

XIV. *Anthroposophische Menschenkunde und Pädagogik,* 9 Public Lectures, various cities, 1923–24 (GA 304a). ***Waldorf Education and Anthroposophy II*** (Anthroposophic Press, 1996).

XV. *Die geistig-seelischen Grundkräfte der Erziehungskunst,* 12 Lectures, 1 Special Lecture, Oxford 1922 (GA 305). ***The Spiritual Ground of Education*** (Anthroposophic Press, 1996).

XVI. *Die pädagogisch Praxis vom Gesichtspunkte geisteswissenschaftlicher Menschenerkenntnis,* 8 Lectures, Dornach, 1923 (GA 306). ***The Child's Changing Consciousness as the Basis of Pedagogical Practice*** (Anthroposophic Press, 1996).

XVII. *Gegenwärtiges Geistesleben und Erziehung,* 4 Lectures, Ilkeley, 1923 (GA 307). ***A Modern Art of Education*** (Rudolf Steiner Press, 1981) and ***Education and Modern Spiritual Life*** (Garber Publications, n.d.).

XVIII. *Die Methodik des Lehrens und die Lebensbedingungen des Erziehens,* 5 Lectures, Stuttgart, 1924 (GA 308). ***The Essentials of Education*** (Rudolf Steiner Press, 1968).

XIX. *Anthroposophische Pädagogik und ihre Voraussetzungen,* 5 Lectures, Bern, 1924 (GA 309). ***The Roots of Education*** (Rudolf Steiner Press, 1968).

XX. *Der pädagogische Wert der Menschenerkenntnis und der Kulturwert der Pädagogik,* 10 Public Lectures, Arnheim, 1924 (GA 310). ***Human Values in Education*** (Rudolf Steiner Press, 1971).

XXI. *Die Kunst des Erziehens aus dem Erfassen der Menschenwesenheit,* 7 Lectures, Torquay, 1924 (GA 311). ***The Kingdom of Childhood*** (Anthroposophic Press, 1995).

XXII. *Geisteswissenschaftliche Impulse zur Entwicklung der Physik. Erster naturwissenschaftliche Kurs: Licht, Farbe, Ton—Masse, Elektrizität, Magnetismus,* 10 Lectures, Stuttgart, 1919–20 (GA 320). ***The Light Course*** (Steiner Schools Fellowship,1977).

XXIII. *Geisteswissenschaftliche Impulse zur Entwicklung der Physik. Zweiter naturwissenschaftliche Kurs: die Wärme auf der Grenze positiver und negativer Materialität,* 14 Lectures, Stuttgart, 1920 (GA 321). ***The Warmth Course*** (Mercury Press, 1988).

XXIV. *Das Verhältnis der verschiedenen naturwissenschaftlichen Gebiete zur Astronomie. Dritter naturwissenschaftliche Kurs: Himmelskunde in Beziehung zum Menschen und zur Menschenkunde,* 18 Lectures, Stuttgart, 1921 (GA 323). Available in typescript only as "**The Relation of the Diverse Branches of Natural Science to Astronomy**."

XXV. ***The Education of the Child and Early Lectures on Education*** (A collection) (Anthroposophic Press, 1996).

XXVI. Miscellaneous.

Index

DURING THE LAST TWO DECADES of the nineteenth century the Austrian-born Rudolf Steiner (1861–1925) became a respected and well-published scientific, literary, and philosophical scholar, particularly known for his work on Goethe's scientific writings. After the turn of the century he began to develop his earlier philosophical principles into an approach to methodical research of psychological and spiritual phenomena.

His multifaceted genius has led to innovative and holistic approaches in medicine, science, education (Waldorf schools), special education, philosophy, religion, economics, agriculture (Biodynamic method), architecture, drama, new arts of eurythmy and speech, and other fields. In 1924 he founded the General Anthroposophical Society, which today has branches throughout the world.